MICHAEL COREN

WHY CATHOLICS ARE RIGHT

McClelland & Stewart

Library and Archives Canada Cataloguing in Publication

Coren, Michael
Why Catholics are right / Michael Coren.

Also issued in electronic format.
ISBN 978-0-7710-2321-7

1. Catholic Church--Doctrines. 2. Catholic Church--History.
I. Title.

BX1754.C67 2011   230'.2   C2010-905282-X

We acknowledge the financial support of the Government of Canada through the Book Publishing Industry Development Program and that of the Government of Ontario through the Ontario Media Development Corporation's Ontario Book Initiative. We further acknowledge the support of the Canada Council for the Arts and the Ontario Arts Council for our publishing program.

Library of Congress Control Number: 2010938559

Typeset in Dante by M&S, Toronto
Printed and bound in Canada

ANCIENT FOREST
FRIENDLY

Every effort has been made to secure permission from the copyright holders of excerpts quoted in this book.

This book is printed on acid-free paper that is 100% recycled, ancient-forest friendly (100% post-consumer waste).

McClelland & Stewart Ltd.
75 Sherbourne Street
Toronto, Ontario
M5A 2P9
www.mcclelland.com

4   5   15   14   13   12   11

C O N T E N T S

INTRODUCTION

WHEN I FIRST TOLD FRIENDS and colleagues about this book, they were intrigued by its proposed content but disturbed by its title. "Sounds a little proud," "Is that sufficiently concilia- tory for these progressive and pluralistic days?" and "You ought to be careful because it might offend people." Which is odd in that when I suggested to them titles for other books such as *Why Liberals Are Right, Why Conservatives Are Right,* even *Why Muslims Are Right,* and especially *Why Atheists Are Right,* they thought the suggestions to describe the various subjects en- tirely reasonable and unlikely to cause any problems at all. To believe something is, self-evidently, not to believe something that is its contrary. So obvious is this that it is not questioned and seems a self-evident truth in most areas and about most subjects. It is, after all, just common sense. But to claim that being an authentic Roman Catholic necessitates believing that Roman Catholicism is correct positively terrifies many modern men and women, as though a Catholic claiming to be right was some terrible sin – not that many of these people believe in sin, of course.

If this audacious insistence that being Catholic meant, well, being Catholic and led to the persecution or killing of others who were not Catholic, it would naturally be intimidat- ing and insulting but that is certainly not the case – even though, as we will see in the first chapter, it usually takes only a few mo- ments during a disagreement for someone to bring up the days when Catholics did indeed give their opponents a hard time, as though in all of history only Catholics have ever got it wrong or even just acted like most people were acting at the time.

So the title stands, and for a specific reason: to oblige and demand a certain clarity on the part of the book's readers. I'm a Catholic and believe in Catholicism, and thus I believe that people who disagree with my beliefs are wrong. I do not dislike them – or at least don't dislike all of them – nor do I wish to hurt them, even those who wish to hurt me and will probably wish to hurt me even more after they read this book, pretend to read it, or read nasty reviews of it.

I do, however, want these readers to consider what I have to say and to not abuse my beliefs in a manner and with a harshness that they would not dream of using against almost any other creed or religion. It might be a romantic hope but hope is one of those Catholic qualities we like to think of as important and helpful.

Having said this, I admit there are degrees of wrongness. Some people are only slightly wrong, others wrong most of the time and to a shocking degree. Non-Catholic Christians and in particular serious evangelicals and Eastern Orthodox believers are examples of the former. Many of them could teach many Catholics a great deal about love, charity, and devotion to God. Alleged Christians who want to edit rather than follow Christ, professional atheists who flood the Internet with their obsessions, and part-time Catholic-bashers are the latter. This brings me to the anti-Catholicism that has become the last acceptable prejudice in what passes for polite society and has become so obvious and so pronounced that to even repeat the fact seems almost banal. We have all heard comments about Catholics that if applied to almost any other group would simply not be tolerated. It's bad enough when this is street conversation and pointless gossip, far worse when it passes for informed comment in allegedly serious newspapers. British historian and biographer Christopher Hibbert put it well when he said that historically the Pope had been thought of as "an unseen, ghost-like enemy, lurking behind clouds of wicked incense in a Satanic southern city called Rome." In much of contemporary Anglo-Saxon culture as well as the greater modern world, this perverse caricature has found a second wind.

Philip Jenkins is a professor of history and religion at Pennsylvania State University and has written extensively about the Roman Catholic Church and some of the attacks on it. His book *The New Anti-Catholicism: The Last Acceptable Prejudice*[1] outlined the history and modern experience of the phenomenon. Jenkins himself left the Church in the 1980s. When his book was published, he was asked to define its thesis. He replied, "It depends on how you define anti-Catholicism. I suggest it is a very widespread phenomenon in different degrees. For example, people would say things about the Catholic Church and condemn a religion with much more ease than they would condemn other religions, other religious traditions. I think that's always been true to some extent, but I think that's really shifted its basis in the last twenty-five years. It's become much more of a left-liberal, as opposed to a right-wing prerogative." He continued, "It makes anti-Catholicism different from other kinds of prejudice. It survives as what I call 'the last acceptable prejudice.' In other words, if you say something that is insensitive or hostile about most religious or ethnic groups, then those words will come back to haunt you and in many cases destroy you. . . . If you say something about Catholicism, or even something which is very hostile, really quite extreme, and in many people's idea, constitutes outrageous bigotry, it doesn't.

Nobody really notices. You're expected to lighten up and not take this too seriously."[2]

Jenkins is right. And this is all far more profound than merely responding to an achingly nasty and smothering bigotry. The importance of Catholicism is that in a culture where various forms of religious and atheistic fundamentalism, crass materialism, and clawing decadence eat away at civility and civilization the only permanent, consistent, and logically complete alternative is the Roman Catholic Church. Which is probably why it seems to so antagonize people who would usually be fair and tolerant toward a faith or ideology they did not completely understand.

I was not born a Catholic and came into the Church only in my mid-twenties. I'd grown up in a secular home in Britain with a Jewish father whose family had fled Poland in the 1890s. He wasn't anti-Catholic but he saw the Church as something foreign and alien, from both a Jewish and a British perspective. While London in the 1960s and 1970s was hardly anti-Semitic to any meaningful degree, it's impossible to have Jewish blood and not experience at least some prejudice and hatred. Even if it isn't direct and personal, it's a ghost that haunts the world, and, with the growth of both the Internet and the nuances of Middle Eastern politics and an increasing distance from the Holocaust, it has been given new life in recent years. So I know what being despised simply for being is all about. Anti-Catholicism is fundamentally different from anti-Semitism. It's not racial or ethnic and, outside of fundamentalist Protestant circles and Islamic extremists, not even especially religious. Very few people dislike Catholicism because of its theology but many oppose it because of the moral and ethical consequences of its teachings. In spite of that, in 2008 the Internet video-sharing website YouTube hosted forty videos showing the graphic desecration of the consecrated host. They had been posted by an anti-Catholic activist who was seen burning, nailing, and stapling the Eucharist and flushing it down a toilet.

This is obviously incredibly offensive to Catholics who, as we shall see, believe the consecrated host to be the body and blood of Jesus Christ. Perhaps so, runs the standard response, but while Catholics are entitled to their opinion, those who disagree with them are allowed theirs and may be as offensive as they like as long as they do not use violence. The problem is that this approach seems to be applied to Christians and Catholics in particular far more than to others. Robert Ritchie was the director of an organization called America Needs Fatima, which compiled petitions to try to have the videos removed. He explained, "As Catholics, we believe the host is the body, blood, soul, and divinity of Christ. Witnessing the desecration of the host causes anguish to Catholics all over the world. In the past, YouTube has removed videos offensive to Jews and members of other religions, including one showing a teenager urinating on a Holocaust memorial. Why can't Catholics be afforded the same respect for our deeply held beliefs?" The argument can be extended to any number of areas where Catholicism is treated differently from other faiths.

But in general, religious anti-Catholicism is fairly unusual. In other words, I've seldom met someone who dislikes me because of my views on saints or the papacy, but I have lost jobs in media because of my Catholic belief that, for example, life begins at conception and that marriage can only be between one man and one woman. Being part Jewish, on the other hand, has positively helped me in my career, whereas my serious Catholicism has led to at least two firings and many doors in media being closed. So while anti-Semitism is vile and constant, being an observant Catholic, at least in the Western world, can lead to other different but equally difficult problems.

There is evidently an anti-Catholic prejudice that is built on social and economic grounds. In Britain, for example, Catholics were often Irish immigrants and just as often working class and even poor. Although Roman Catholicism was the faith of the British for a thousand years, by the early seventeenth century it had been pushed to the fringes of society. In Northern Ireland, there were and to an extent still are Protestants who regard Catholics as morally as well as personally and theologically inferior. In North America, some of that Anglo-Celtic prejudice still exists – the Catholic Church is, in popular and sometimes even cultured circles, regarded as the "denomination of foreigners, immigrants, the poor, and undesirables" – but the bulk of modern contemporary disdain comes more often from the secular liberal who feels intellectually and aesthetically superior but would never dare feel such contempt for a member of a more fashionable minority group.

Catholics also face the problem of dislike from those once their own. The notion of "once a Catholic" is problematic because if someone aggressively rejects Catholicism, they are patently no longer Catholic. A Jew may embrace atheism but still be Jewish. Catholicism is different. A Catholic who becomes, say, a Baptist is not a Catholic and it would be insulting to claim otherwise. The problem is that many people raised nominally or even devoutly Catholic who then turn against the Church want the best, or worst, of both worlds and continue to attack the faith while still claiming to be of it. One malicious term – "recovering Catholic" – is supposed to equate Catholicism with alcoholism or drug addiction. I prefer "failed Catholic," which for some reason rather annoys those self-identified "recovering Catholics" who obsess about how difficult their life was until they discovered the liberation of Buddhism, New Age, or atheism.

This book is not supposed to be anything like a definitive guide to Roman Catholicism. It is a mere handbook dealing with some of the most common but by no means all of the attacks on the Church and should be useful to Catholics who want to defend their beliefs but need a little help, an intellectualizing of the instinctive or a mild fleshing out of what they already thought to be the case. It should also be of use to honestly curious non-Catholics who have heard the usual accusations and rumours and can't believe that this institution that has done so much good and contains so many good people can truly be so evil and wrong. I mean the sort of people who are too intelligent and mature to believe in fairy tales. I hope it leads some to read further and deeper, to look at modern Catholic authors and apologists as well as some of the greats of the nineteenth century and even of the medieval age. There are any number of questions, areas, and issues that I have not addressed and all sorts of facts, figures, and arguments that I have not explored – the book is intended to be accessible rather than exhaustive. More space is devoted to the more frequent criticisms of the Church than to areas that may be important but for various reasons are not usually targets of abuse. Roman Catholics are far more likely, for example, to be attacked for what people assume are the facts about the Crusades than they are about the Immaculate Conception, more likely to face challenges about the Church's alleged indifference to the Holocaust and supposed obsession with abortion than about purgatory or the nonsense that there was a female Pope. Lady pontiffs and the Immaculate Conception, by the way, are covered but not to the same extent as the Crusades and the Holocaust.

The book is written out of experience as well as research. What I mean is that my experience has taught me that attacks usually begin with the Church's history, then with a misunderstanding of what the Church believes and teaches, then with angry comments about why the Church is so "obsessed" with the life issue and then a whole bunch of criticisms. These days, tragically, the Catholic clergy abuse scandal is thrown in somewhere. It has to be discussed, but it has to be discussed honestly and accurately. The rest of the punches thrown at the Catholic body? The Church was nasty to Galileo, the Church tried to convert Muslims and the Crusades were horrible, Hitler was a Catholic and the Pope was a Nazi, the Inquisition slaughtered millions of people, the Church is rich and does nothing for the poor, children were abused and the Vatican knew about it all and did nothing, celibacy leads to perversion, Catholics worship statues, Catholics believe the Pope is infallible and can never do anything wrong, and so on and so on and so on.

It's all nonsense – yet it's nonsense that is given a veneer of credibility by thinking people who shape opinion, which, again, makes the Church unique in the twenty-first century as a victim institution. In almost every other area, we've matured as a people and a culture to the point where such crass generalizations and fundamentally flawed opinions would not make it past the alehouse door. Not with Roman Catholicism. This is a small book about a huge subject, but that should not detract from its premise that Catholicism is right and this is why. Read and think, think and agree, think and disagree, think whatever you like. But in the name of God and the Church He left us, please think!

CATHOLICS
AND THE
ABUSE SCANDAL

THIS IS THE CHAPTER that I didn't want to write and shouldn't have to. It's the chapter most people would rather not have to read. If only it were redundant and unnecessary and we could get on with the genuine issues – which is not to say that the Roman Catholic clergy abuse scandal was and is irrelevant or did not happen. Far from it. Thousands of people, mainly adolescent young men, were smashed, destroyed, broken, abused, raped, assaulted by criminals and perverts who hid their disorders, their cowardice, and their criminality beneath the sacrament of the priesthood. Not only were the direct victims devastated by what happened but so too were their families and friends and the millions of Catholics, and in particular the overwhelming majority of clergy, who live as faithful, good, and honest men and women trying their best to worship God, help others, and repair the wounds of the world. What we have to do for the sake of the victims, the Church, and sheer justice and the truth is to give an authentic account of what happened without whitewashing events but also without using the horror as an excuse to attack the Roman Catholic Church.

Indeed, one of the secondary tragedies of what has happened in the past few years and what will surely have a ripple effect in years to come has been the neglect of the victims by

11

critics who seem intent not on caring for the injured but on exploiting the suffering of these poor people to attack the Church. While there are victims who are understandably angry at the Church and who now refuse to call themselves Catholic, there are also abused Catholics who still love their faith and know that their experiences were the result not of the Church but of people within it who failed to lead a genuinely Catholic life. If only these saints could be listened to a little more often rather than the Church being shouted at all the time. People do bad things in the name of good causes, have done so throughout history, and will continue to do so. People kill and lie in the name of, for example, democracy, love, and peace but that does not mean that democracy, love, or peace are inherently evil. The Church is composed of people, and people do terrible things and commit sin – it's what the Church has been telling us for two thousand years and continues to tell us, which is why the Church is here and essentially one of the major reasons why people hate it so much.

We have to be specific with facts and outline the truth, no matter how cold or clinical it may sound. The rates of sexual abuse within the Roman Catholic Church were in the past exactly the same as those in other Christian churches and within other faith communities, though they may well be lower now. More than this, they were on a par with the abuse rates within any institution involving a power ratio between adult and young person, such as education, sports teams, and so on.[1] All these incidents are deeply tragic. But to single one of these bodies out for particular venom seems strange. Of course, the Church speaks with a moral authority not claimed by a sports club or a school, so in this regard it is right that the Church should be particularly exposed, but the condemnation went much further than justified criticism and became dishonest, libellous, and hysterical. Horrible as it is to contemplate, the most dangerous place for a young person with regard to sexual abuse is the family, often with young women being abused by stepfathers or stepbrothers. Today the Catholic Church is probably the safest place for a young boy or girl because of what the Church has done to make it so. This is in no way to adopt the odious "it's not just us" approach but to show that abuse is not peculiar to the Church and says nothing specific about Catholicism.[2]

If we look at the situation in the United States within other religious groups and various secular bodies, we see a revealing if disturbing picture, and the United States is entirely typical of the international experience. In Protestant circles, for example, a 1984 survey showed that 38.6 per cent of ministers reported some sort of sexual contact with a member of the church and 76 per cent claimed to know of another minister who had had sexual intercourse with someone who attended the church.[3] Nor is this confined to one particular branch of the Protestant Church but seems to pervade liberal, mainstream, and orthodox denominations. The highly respected Fuller Seminary conducted an extensive survey of 1,200 ministers and concluded that 20 per cent of conservative pastors admitted to a sexual relationship outside of marriage with a member of the church, with the figure doubling to an extraordinary 40 per cent for self-identified moderate ministers – the numbers rise to a staggering 50 per cent for so-called liberals.[4] How much of this behaviour concerns minors is uncertain but the number is likely to be relatively low. Professor Philip Jenkins estimates that between 2 and 3 per cent of Protestant clergy have abused minors, but he puts the figure for Catholic priests at less than 2 per cent. Jenkins, remember, is a former Catholic who is now an Anglican and is far from being a Roman Catholic apologist.[5] In 2002, the *Christian Science Monitor,* not a particular friend or supporter of Catholicism, reported on the results of national surveys conducted by an organization called Christian Ministry Resources and stated that, "despite headlines focusing on the priest pedophile problem in the Roman Catholic Church, most American churches being hit with child sexual-abuse allegations are Protestant, and most of the alleged abusers are not clergy or staff, but church volunteers."[6]

Beyond the Christian faith, Rabbi Arthur Gross Schaefer, professor of law and ethics at Loyola Marymount University, believes that sexual abuse among rabbis within organized Judaism is roughly the same as that found within Protestant clergy. "Sadly," says Rabbi Schaefer, "our community's reactions up to this point have been often based on keeping things quiet in an attempt to do damage control. Fear of lawsuits and bad publicity have dictated an atmosphere of hushed voices and outrage against those who dare to break ranks by speaking out."[7] In the field of education, the American Medical Association found in 1986 that one in four girls and one in eight boys were sexually abused in or out of school before the age of 18.[8] In the city of New York alone, at least one child is sexually abused by a school employee every day![9] In 1994, Hofstra University professor Charol Shakeshaft conducted a study of 225 cases of educator sexual abuse in New York City and found that although every one of the accused admitted to sexual abuse of a student, not one of the abusers was reported to the authorities, and only 1 per cent of the abusers lost their licence to teach.

In 2001, the National Child Abuse and Neglect Data System developed by the Children's Bureau in the United States found that approximately 903,000 children were victims of maltreatment, and 10 per cent of them (or a little more than 90,000) were sexually abused. It also found that 59 per cent of the perpetrators of child abuse or neglect were women and 41 per cent were men, statistics that reflect international findings. In the same year, clinical child psychologist Wade F. Horn wrote a report on the work of researchers at Johns Hopkins University School of Public Health, where it was shown that nearly 20 per cent of low-income women in their study had experienced sexual abuse as children, with family friends constituting the largest group of abusers, followed by uncles and cousins, then stepfathers, and then brothers.

Which is all pretty depressing stuff and, again, must not be used to somehow explain away the Catholic scandal just because evil, exploitation, and abuse is a theme in almost every area of society. What this does show is that those critics who seemed to be so morbidly eager to prove that abuse was all about Catholicism, about Catholic teaching, and about Catholic sexuality were completely wrong and never made a worthy attempt to put the horror in any sort of valuable context. So at its most clinical, we need to describe the abuse crisis that happened within the Church primarily but not exclusively in the 1960s and 1970s. In this period, between 1.5 and 4 per cent of Roman Catholic clergy were involved directly or indirectly in the abuse of young people under their authority. The figure includes those who may not have physically abused anyone but were aware in some way of the abuse and by not stopping it enabled it and allowed the abusers to repeat the offence. Most informed commentators think that the 4 per cent figure is far too high, but we will never know the exact number of victims because not every victim has come forward, for a variety of entirely understandable reasons. Most of the abused were boys between the ages of twelve and sixteen, but younger boys and girls were also molested. Although the term "pedophile priests" was and is commonly used, it is misleading and sometimes appears to be intended to mislead. A crime, of course, is a crime, but if we are to deal with the perpetrators properly and try to stop the crime being repeated, we need to understand its precise nature and stop dealing in tabloid terminology and sensational headlines. Alliteration is no substitute for accuracy.

Pedophilia involves the sexual attraction of men (there are women pedophiles but they are rare) to children who do not resemble adults and have not yet reached puberty. Any exploration of pedophilia reveals the most distressing crimes; young children are kidnapped and assaulted, babies are touched and suffer unimaginable obscenities. The ages of the victims vary because there are pedophiles who are attracted to different stages of childhood, be it a five-year-old, eight-year-old, or even, heaven cries out, newborn infants. What occurred in the Catholic Church was generally something different – men forcing sex on boys who were sexually developed but underage and emotionally and physically vulnerable. Because this was not pedophilia does not excuse it in any way whatsoever – it is a hideous crime. But we have to call it what it was and is and not mangle the truth for the sake of political correctness or confused sensitivities.

According to the *Washington Post* – hardly a friend of the Church – since 1965 less than 1.5 per cent of the more than 60,000 priests working in the United States have ever been accused of any form of sexual abuse, and the *New York Times,* even less of a friend, estimates that 1.8 per cent of priests ordained between 1950 and 2001 have faced any abuse-related charges. Obviously these figures have to be understood in the light of some abusers never being discovered and some of the abuse never being reported. We also have to remind ourselves, painful though it may be, that there have also been false allegations, and innocent men have had their lives ruined by unscrupulous people exploiting the pain and suffering of others who genuinely have been assaulted. The reaction of bishops and the Church hierarchy and establishment when abuse was alleged or proven varied, but when we look back on it all, we can say with some confidence that it was seldom successful and sometimes downright wrong. There were some men, albeit a small minority, in positions of authority in the Church who were themselves abusers or sexual allies of the abusers and allowed the crimes to continue. Others were simply incompetent or unqualified and tried to do their best in a situation they had not encountered before and found utterly shocking. Most bishops demanded that the abuse stop immediately, insisted that the abuser undergo prolonged counselling, and moved the offender elsewhere in an attempt to break the abuse cycle and allow the victim to move on. Looking back on this approach, we cringe or shake our heads in disbelief. It seems so archaic, so naïve, and so certain to fail and allow the abuser to continue his crimes. Yet this was typical of the era and was the standard advice given by experts not only to churches but to school boards, sports teams, and any other institution where such abuse occurred. It's anachronistic and unfair to expect a modern, sophisticated approach to abuse cases from the Catholic Church of, for example, the 1970s, when the sexual therapists and psychiatrists who were advising Church leaders were also advising similar policies to secular bodies where abuse rates were the same or higher and where teachers, coaches, and the like were also reprimanded, given counselling, and reassigned. It may fulfil an agenda to paint the Church as being appallingly behind the times and callow in the area of sexuality, but it doesn't help us get any closer to the truth. What it does do is allow critics of the Church to claim that it's all part of a greater crisis and one that is based on fundamental Church teaching, doctrine, and discipline.

This point of view is why the attacks on the Church regarding the abuse issue invariably jump after a few steps to two major premises: celibacy led to the sexual abuse scandal, and an all-male clergy made the abuse far more likely to occur and then to be hidden. I will deal with the theological reasons why priests are male and celibate at the end of the chapter, but at a purely logical level this is obviously ridiculous. As already mentioned, the abuse levels in churches and non-religious bodies where men and women are in positions of power and where celibacy is not required are little different from, and sometimes higher than, those in the Catholic Church in the 60s and 70s. So neither factor can be of any influence, unless the person drawing the conclusion is more concerned with bombarding Catholic teaching than with dealing with the causes of the rape of young boys. It also defies common sense and any understanding of male sexuality to assume that normal men become attracted to thirteen-year-old boys because they are sexually frustrated and have been chaste since entering the seminary. Celibacy might explain a normal man's attraction to an adult woman, but homosexual arousal occurs only within homosexuals and homosexual arousal by adolescent minors occurs only within homosexuals attracted to adolescent minors. It's not that difficult to understand if we listen rather than shout. Whether we like to admit it or not, the majority of abusers who were Catholic clergy self-identified as homosexual, and most of the offences were of a homosexual nature. This does not mean and must not lead people to believe that homosexual men are more likely to abuse than heterosexual men – there is no evidence for this at all and, anyway, it obscures the point. Not all homosexual men abuse, but most of the men abusing in this crisis were homosexual men. They were likely homosexual when they entered the seminary; they either used the priesthood as a cover for their sexual desires or gave in to temptation at some point during or after their time at the seminary.

The figures, however difficult they are to accept, are beyond dispute. Santa Clara University psychologist Dr. Thomas Plante estimates that "80 to 90% of all priests who in fact abuse minors have sexually engaged with adolescent boys, not prepubescent children. Thus, the teenager is more at risk than the young altar boy or girls of any age." In the United States, some of the worst scandals occurred in Boston and according to the *Boston Globe*, "Of the clergy sex abuse cases referred to prosecutors in Eastern Massachusetts, more than 90 percent involve male victims. And the most prominent Boston lawyers for alleged victims of clergy sexual abuse have said that about 95 percent of their clients are male." In research *USA Today* undertook of 1,200 victims abused by priests, 85 per cent were boys; the same newspaper concluded that of the 234 priests accused of abuse in the ten largest diocese in the United States, 91 per cent of the victims were male.[11]

Most people, gay or straight, are, naturally, disgusted at what occurred and appreciate, as should we all, that sexuality and crime have no rigid connection. Those who abuse, lie, and exploit do so because of their immorality and not because of their sexual preference. When, however, the Church came to understand the nature of the crisis and made it far more difficult for homosexual men to become priests – it is the act and not the temptation that is important, but if the temptation to a particular sin is too great it has to be taken into account by a candidate to the seminary – it was immediately accused of homophobia by many of the same people who had accused it of not doing enough to protect young people from predator clergy. In other words, the Church was damned if it did and damned if it didn't; then again, for its critics it was damned long ago. It's an open wound and one that causes excruciating torment, but most of the sweeping statements surrounding this scandal lack nuance and have tended to come from the Church's critics and not from the Church itself.

In fact, the media hyperbole and sheer lack of information and objectivity concerning the crisis were perhaps unprecedented in modern reporting. In 2010, journalist Bob Ellis, for example, wrote a piece for ABC Australia that was admittedly on the extreme end of the coverage but was by no means unusual. "No one has yet suggested bombing the Vatican and pursuing the Pope through the sewers of Europe till he is caught and riddled with bullets in order to stop priests buggering choirboys in Boston, Chicago, Dublin and Sydney," he wrote. "But a precise mirror image of this is how we behaved in Afghanistan. If we bomb it flat, we were told, and pursue Bin Laden through the caves of Tora Bora and the mud huts of Waziristan until he is caught and riddled with bullets, al-Qaeda won't hijack planes and blow up trains any more. And the world will live at peace. We were told this eight years ago. And we believed it."

He continued, "Let's consider for a while the comparable crimes, or iniquities, or sins, or misdeeds, or culpable errors of Osama bin Laden and the Pope. Osama's followers killed 3,000 people in New York and around 700 more by terrorist acts in

London, Bali, Madrid and Mumbai in the past eight years and desolated maybe 20,000 lives of the relatives of the dead. The Pope's followers desolated, perhaps, 100,000 lives (or this is my guess) by sexual depravity in the past 80 years and killed, perhaps, (this too is my guess, I ask for yours) no more than 5,000 smashed and embittered Catholic boys and girls they drove to suicide or drunken oblivion and early death in those years."

On a roll now and obviously relishing the moment, he concluded, "The crimes are comparable pretty much and well-attested and well known from enquiries here and in Germany, the US and Ireland. Why then do we not bomb the Vatican and obliterate Italy for harbouring this criminal mastermind, this known protector of evil predators? Why do we not pursue him through the sewers of Europe and riddle his corpse with bullets? Why are we not bombing the Vatican? One wonders now what should be done with buggering priests and those that hide them from our detection. Clearly bombing Italy and Ireland is an insufficient solution, to judge by what little effect our bombing and rocketing and random arrest and rendition to houses of torture have had on the Taliban thus far and their hold on the minds of their people. Yet precisely this kind of crime has occurred in another institution responsible for the care and shaping of children, the Catholic Church. Should it be outlawed? Catholics too? Why not bomb the Vatican, and riddle the Pope with bullets as he staggers out of the flames?"

Hardly a shining episode of reasoned debate and not conducive to a civilized discussion of a delicate and painful issue. This is a clumsy and ham-fisted attempt to criticize Western foreign policy while simultaneously accusing the Church of crimes it did not commit and making it appear as inherently evil. We saw such twisted thinking and destructive anger all over the world, as though editing and the usual demands of self-restraint and honest reporting no longer applied when the Catholic Church was the subject of a column or even news article. This is one man, it's true, but the coverage of the abuse scandal by the highly esteemed *New York Times* was often just as bad. The newspaper was even obliged to correct some of the accusations it had made about the Church at Easter 2010 – it appears that Christmas and Easter have become favourite seasons now for the mainstream media to attack Roman Catholicism. On March 25, the *Times* reported, "Top Vatican officials – including the future Pope Benedict xvi – did not defrock a priest who molested as many as 200 deaf boys, even though several American bishops repeatedly warned them that failure to act on the matter could embarrass the church, according to church files newly unearthed as part of a lawsuit."

Where to start? Actually, the case against Father Lawrence Murphy, the priest in question, was initiated by the "top Vatican officials," was never stopped, and was ongoing when Murphy died. Cardinal Ratzinger, the future Pope Benedict, is not shown in the documents to have taken any decisions in this case at all, and the actual culprit, aside from Murphy himself, was the former Archbishop of Milwaukee, Rembert Weakland, who was also a published source for the story. This is dreadful stuff and dreadful journalism because Weakland resigned in disgrace in 2002 after it was revealed that he had been conducting a homosexual affair and had used $450,000 of archdiocesan funds in an attempt to bribe his lover into secrecy. He had also had other homosexual relationships, had mismanaged abuse cases, and was brutally opposed to Pope Benedict because of the Pope's orthodoxy and determination to enforce sexual purity in the Church. All of this should have made Weakland an unreliable witness and an awful source for any newspaper story, especially one involving such dramatic and damaging allegations. Instead, it seemed to increase the man's standing in the eyes of the *New York Times*.

This, again, was entirely typical of some newspapers and television stations and became the norm for much of the coverage of the issue. Previously respected columnists asked in self-righteously accusing tones why the Church allowed this to happen, demanded to know when it would put its house in order, and showed how noble they were by insisting on an answer when asking the Church why it hadn't apologized. But the Church had apologized, over and over again. The Pope had begged forgiveness, spoke of "cleansing the filth" from the Church, and new guidelines and regulations were put in place all over the Catholic world. This has not, sadly, been the case with other influential international organizations. In 2004, the United Nations, for example, announced a zero-tolerance policy for sex abusers among its peacekeeping troops because of what the under-secretary-general for peacekeeping operations, Alain le Roy, told the *Wall Street Journal* was his "biggest headache and heartache, this whole issue." In Haiti, Cambodia, West Africa, and Kosovo between 2007 and 2010 alone, 75 peacekeepers were disciplined for sexual misconduct, but it is estimated that the problem is enormous and the action taken trivial. In 2009, only 14 of 82 requests for information from the UN involving sexual abuse were answered. According to Jordan's Prince Zeid Ra'ad Zeid Al-Hussein, who authored the 2005 report on the issue, "There is a natural instinct to basically cover up the whole thing. You don't want your name sullied or your reputation affected and so you try and bury it." The UN fails while the Church succeeds, but only one of those bodies receives such constant criticism over the abuse issue.

The situation is similar with something as ostensibly innocent and non-political or controversial as sport. ABC Television in the United States found that thirty-six swimming coaches – out of twelve thousand – have been banned for life for sexual misconduct since 2000 by USA Swimming. ABC claimed that "in some cases, the swimming coaches found to have been sexual predators were able to move from town to town, one step ahead of police and angry victims and their parents." The same pathology has been repeated in soccer and hockey and other sports in Europe, Canada, the United States, and the United Kingdom.

All of this is tragic and repugnant, but these are aberrations within a greater entity; in other words, there is general outrage when the crimes occur but we know that most sports coaches, most soldiers, most people, are not abusers. Mind you, horror is not always the response to cases of sexual abuse of young people – and it is always abuse because youngsters cannot give consent in any meaningful sense – and there are people who genuinely believe that sex between men and young people is acceptable and even healthy. In 1977, the French newspaper *Le Monde* published an open letter signed by sixty-nine French intellectuals, including Jack Lang, a future minister for culture and minister for education, and Bernard Kouchner, a future minister for health and president of Médecins Sans Frontières, along with luminaries such as Jean-Paul Sartre, Gilles Deleuze, and Roland Barthes. They were protesting the imprisonment of three men accused of having sex with thirteen- and fourteen-year-olds. Ministers Lang and Kouchner have both been strong critics of the Roman Catholic Church and its handling of the abuse crisis.

In 2010, the *Huffington Post* in the United States managed a bit of, how shall we say, intellectual schizophrenia. The influential Internet journal boasted headlines throughout the abuse scandal that were positively acid, such as "Vatican Chooses to Prey on Rather Than Pray for Children." On January 1, 2010, it published an article by bioethicist Jacob M. Appel entitled "Embracing Teenage Sexuality: Let's Rethink the Age of Consent." "These draconian and puritanical laws are largely the product of a conservative political culture that has transformed the fight against child molestation into a full-blown war on teenage sexuality," Appel wrote. "We now live in a moral milieu so toxic and muddled that we lump together as sex offenders teenagers who send nude photos to each other with clergymen who rape toddlers. A first step toward reversing this madness – and actually protecting the health and safety of teenagers – would be to revise the age of consent downward. . . ." Perhaps prayer no longer applied.

The abuse scandal in Ireland that was revealed in 2009 and 2010 was particularly disturbing due to its extent and because of the influence of the Church in that country. As late as the summer of 2010, Irish journalists were condemning the Pope for his silence on the issue and asking, as with their North American comrades, when he was going to apologize for what had happened. In fact, the Pope had written a long letter to the Irish Church as early as March 2010. This came after prolonged reform of the church in Ireland, prosecution of criminals, removal of priests, and the introduction of practices intended to prevent further abuse. To some critics of Catholicism, the letter may as well never have existed as it simply didn't fit in with their caricature of an indifferent papacy unconcerned with the suffering of the vulnerable. Actually it said, among other things:

"Dear Brothers and Sisters of the Church in Ireland, it is with great concern that I write to you as Pastor of the universal

Church. Like yourselves, I have been deeply disturbed by the information which has come to light regarding the abuse of children and vulnerable young people by members of the Church in Ireland, particularly by priests and religious. I can only share in the dismay and the sense of betrayal that so many of you have experienced on learning of these sinful and criminal acts and the way Church authorities in Ireland dealt with them.

"No one imagines that this painful situation will be resolved swiftly. Real progress has been made, yet much more remains to be done. Perseverance and prayer are needed, with great trust in the healing power of God's grace. . . . At the same time, I must also express my conviction that, in order to recover from this grievous wound, the Church in Ireland must first acknowledge before the Lord and before others the serious sins committed against defenceless children. Such an acknowledgement, accompanied by sincere sorrow for the damage caused to these victims and their families, must lead to a concerted effort to ensure the protection of children from similar crimes in the future.

"As you take up the challenges of this hour, I ask you to remember 'the rock from which you were hewn.' (Is 51:1) Reflect upon the generous, often heroic, contributions made by past generations of Irish men and women to the Church and to humanity as a whole, and let this provide the impetus for honest self-examination and a committed programme of ecclesial and individual renewal. It is my prayer that, assisted by the intercession of her many saints and purified through penance, the Church in Ireland will overcome the present crisis and become once more a convincing witness to the truth and the goodness of Almighty God, made manifest in his Son Jesus Christ."

Writing in the *New York Times*, John Allen, the doyen of

Vatican correspondents, who is respected by critics as well as supporters of the Church due to his balanced and layered reporting, stated that Pope Benedict was "a major chapter in the solution." He continued, "After being elected Pope, Benedict made the abuse cases a priority. One of his first acts was to discipline two high-profile clerics against whom sex abuse allegations had been hanging around for decades, but had previously been protected at the highest levels. He is also the first pope ever to meet with victims of abuse, which he did in the United States and Australia in 2008. He spoke openly about the crisis some five times during his 2008 visit to the United States. And he became the first pope to devote an entire document to the sex abuse crisis, his pastoral letter to Ireland."

In Britain in 2010, the then newly appointed Archbishop of Westminster, Vincent Nichols, argued that Pope Benedict was "the one above all else in Rome that has tackled this thing head on." In the *Times* of London he said, "When he was in charge of the Congregation for the Doctrine of the Faith he had important changes made in Church law: the inclusion in canon law of internet offences against children, the extension of child abuse offences to include the sexual abuse of all under 18, the case by case waiving of the statute of limitation and the establishment of a fast-track dismissal from the clerical state for offenders. He is not an idle observer. His actions speak as well as his words." Yet none of this stopped people such as the atheist and self-promoter Christopher Hitchens from writing in *Slate* that the Pope was "obstructing justice on a global scale." Benedict's whole career, he said, "has the stench of evil – a clinging and systematic evil that is beyond the power of exorcism to dispel." This from someone regarded by his atheist and Catholic-basher friends as an original and profound thinker. It is entirely possible to be critical of Pope Benedict but no serious person who has read his books and speeches and studied his views and actions on delicate themes such as anti-Semitism, the Third World, poverty, war, or globalization could regard Hitchens's views on the Pope as anything other than cruel, flippant, or dumb. Yet he is given full pages in reputable newspapers and magazines to give us ever-more repetitive versions of his propaganda.

Former Canadian police officer Sean Murphy worked for some time on an abuse case that led to the conviction of a Catholic priest. He replied to Hitchens on the Catholic Education Resource Centre website and thought the polemicist "remarkably careless in his reading and incompetent in his research." But then a cop who helped convict a criminal and sexual abuser priest could never understand the situation as well as someone who thought it amusing to make a documentary about Mother Teresa called *Sacred Cow.*

Writing in the *Jerusalem Post* in April 2010, the former mayor of New York, Ed Koch, made his views on the scandal abundantly clear and his column is worth quoting in full.

I believe the continuing attacks by the media on the Roman Catholic Church and Pope Benedict xvi have become manifestations of anti-Catholicism. The procession of articles on the same events are, in my opinion, no longer intended to inform, but simply to castigate. The sexual molestation of children, principally boys, is horrendous. This is agreed to by everyone, Catholics, the Church itself, as well as non-Catholics and the media. The pope has on a number of occasions on behalf of the Church admitted fault and asked for forgiveness. For example, *The New York Times* reported on April 18, 2008, that the pope "came face to face with a scandal that has left lasting wounds on the American church Thursday, holding a surprise meeting with several victims of sexual abuse by priests in the Boston area. . . . 'No words of mine could describe the pain and harm inflicted by such abuse,' the Pope said in his homily. 'It is important that those who have suffered be given loving pastoral attention.'"

On March 20, 2010, the *Times* reported that in his eight page pastoral letter to Irish Catholics, the pope wrote, "You have suffered grievously, and I am truly sorry. . . . Your trust has been betrayed and your dignity has been violated." The pope also "criticized Ireland's bishops for 'grave errors of judgment and failures of leadership.'" The primary explanation for the abuse that happened – not to excuse the retention of priests in positions that enabled them to continue to harm children – was the belief that the priests could be cured by psychotherapy, a theory now long discarded by the medical profession. Regrettably, it is also likely that years ago the abuse of children was not taken as seriously as today. Thank God we've progressed on that issue. Many of those in the media who are pounding on the Church and the pope today clearly do it with delight, and some with malice. The reason, I believe, for the constant assaults is that there are many in the media, and some Catholics as well as many in the public, who object to and are incensed by positions the Church holds, including opposition to all abortions, opposition to gay sex and same-sex marriage, retention of celibacy rules for priests, exclusion of women from the clergy, opposition to birth control measures involving condoms and prescription drugs and opposition to civil divorce. My good friend,

John Cardinal O'Connor, once said, "The Church is not a salad bar, from which to pick and choose what pleases you." The Church has the right to demand fulfillment of all of its religious obligations by its parishioners, and indeed a right to espouse its beliefs generally.

I disagree with the Church on all of these positions. Nevertheless, it has a right to hold these views in accordance with its religious beliefs. I disagree with many tenets of Orthodox Judaism – the religion of my birth – and have chosen to follow the tenets of Conservative Judaism, while I attend an Orthodox synagogue. Orthodox Jews, like the Roman Catholic Church, can demand absolute obedience to religious rules. Those declining to adhere are free to leave.

I believe the Roman Catholic Church is a force for good in the world, not evil. Moreover, the existence of one billion, 130 million Catholics worldwide is important to the peace and prosperity of the planet. Of course, the media should report to the public any new facts bearing upon the issue of child molestation, but its objectivity and credibility are damaged when the *New York Times* declines to publish an op-ed offered by New York Archbishop Timothy Dolan on the issue of anti-Catholicism and offers instead to publish a letter to the editor, which is much shorter and less prominent than an op-ed.

I am appalled that, according to the *Times* of April 6, 2010, "Last week, the center-left daily newspaper *La Repubblica* wrote, without attribution that 'certain Catholic circles' believed the criticism of the Church stemmed from 'a New York Jewish lobby.'" The pope should know that some of his fellow priests can be thoughtless or worse in their efforts to help him. If the "certain Catholic circles" were referring to the *Times,* the Pope should know that the publisher, Arthur Sulzberger, Jr., is Episcopalian, having taken the religion of his mother, and its executive editor, Bill Keller, is also a Christian.

Enough is enough. Yes, terrible acts were committed by members of the Catholic clergy. The Church has paid billions to victims in the US and will pay millions, perhaps billions, more to other such victims around the world. It is trying desperately to atone for its past by its admissions and changes in procedures for dealing with pedophile priests. I will close with a paraphrase of the words of Jesus as set forth in John 8:7: He [or she] that is without sin among you, let him [or her] cast the next stone.

This from a source who knows the Church well from his days as a street politician in a heavily Catholic city but does not embrace its views and generally disagrees with them. What Koch expressed was what so many other people already knew – that as this spew of a story evolved, it became increasingly obvious that the attacks on Pope Benedict, who was one of the fiercest opponents of abusers and those who would cover for them, were part of a larger attack on orthodoxy from the secular media and a battle in the war between liberal and conservative Catholics within the Church, although it's increasingly the case that ultra-liberal Catholics are more liberal than Catholic and aren't really in the Church at all, either theologically or even literally; although many people were compassionate and active and merely wanted to make sure that such abuse in the Church did not happen again, others saw the phenomenon as an opportunity to tear down the existing Church and replace it with something far more to their political, moral, and sociological liking. Don't simply blame individual abusers, they argued, but the institution in which the abuser was allowed to operate. It is horribly ironic that it was the more permissive, liberal 1960s with its exploitation of the Second Vatican Council that created the atmosphere in which sexually confused men were allowed into seminaries in which their dysfunctions were not addressed but often positively encouraged.

Unless we understand this internal conflict, we can never appreciate what is truly going on within the Church. Vatican II was supposed to open up some of the metaphorical windows of the Church but instead was used by some people to smash every piece of stained glass they could find. Minor reform and the understanding that some change was necessary was used as a vehicle to try to create a non-Catholic denomination that had little resemblance to the historic Roman Catholic Church. One example is poignant. The council gave permission for the Mass to be said in the vernacular rather than Latin where there was a sufficient call for it. Within five years, it was almost impossible to find a Mass celebrated in Latin. This was not because of a groundswell of popular demand for the vernacular but the result of the agenda and beliefs of a small number of liberal priests and bishops. In the clamour for greater egalitarianism, a self-appointed elite told the masses how to attend Masses. This was a long way from equality, but then a grasp of irony and a genuine commitment to justice have not been key qualities of left-wing Catholics.

The issue of the ordination of women is not as complex as some people would like us to believe and is really one of basic humility. The Church simply does not have the authority to ordain women. It's not a question of what anybody would like or want or even need but an issue of scripture and the teaching of Christ. This might not be important for non-Christians but is extremely relevant to those who worship and follow Jesus Christ. It is interesting, of course, how many who not only don't believe in Christ or God but despise Catholicism seem concerned about changing the Church when it comes to the subject of women clergy. The first and more important fact is that Jesus being born male was not some chance event or an accidental decision. God has a purpose in everything He does. Within the sacrificial system of Israel and the Jewish people, the Sin offering and Passover Lamb had to be males without blemish, and since Christ fulfils these sacrifices He had to be a man. The Church is seen in scripture and tradition as a bride with God as the bridegroom – the roles are there for a reason and out of God's plan for us and for the Church. We don't have to believe in God, but if we do we surely have to believe that He knows more about His plan than we do. In Catholicism, the priest acts in *persona Christi* (in the person of Christ) as Jesus celebrates the sacraments for His bride, the Church, through the actions of the male priest. It is not a question of equality but of divinity.

It has also been argued that Christ was only observing the cultural norms of His day and that two thousand years later we need to adapt just as we have in many other areas where ideas of what is acceptable have changed. Or to put it another way, Jesus was a prisoner of His age and just didn't get it. Apart from the obvious dangers and sheer silliness of such a relativistic approach, the basic premise is fundamentally flawed. Christ ignored or rejected many social and cultural aspects of his time, which is one of the reasons – though not the main one – that He was opposed by the theological and political establishment.

He was not a conformist and had no problem at all with inter-acting with women, much to the annoyance of many of the religious reactionaries of His time. Indeed, not only women but women of dubious reputation and questionable pasts were wel-comed into his group, an inclusion that was positively shock-ing to many of His contemporaries. In numerous other areas, He broke with custom and tradition but chose to observe it as well when it mattered and when it was important and necessary for the plan of salvation to do so – culture and tradition were forced to adapt to Him, not He to them. This is extraordinarily important. Christ ordained only men and chose them as His disciples for precise reasons and not out of some peculiarity or banality of time.

He was also well acquainted with priestesses, who were common in the religions of the era and His homeland, at least outside of Judaism. If He'd wanted to ordain women there was no stronger and more qualified candidate than Mary, who is the only other person who could have spoken the words "This is my body. This is my blood" and been literally accurate. Yet He chose specifically and deliberately to ordain only men, while giving women enormously prominent positions in His ministry and teaching. Catholics are frequently criticised because of the prominence and respect given to the Virgin Mary while simul-taneously condemned for not giving enough prominence and respect to women. While the Pope is, obviously, the Pope and can only be a man, he is not as honoured within Catholicism as the saints and the doctors of the Church. There are hundreds of female saints, many of them the most important and beloved. There are also three women doctors of the Church. If this is misogyny, then the Catholic Church has a lot of learning to do.

Christ's vision for the place of women in the church both

during and after His life on earth is centrally important. It is women who first tell of His resurrection, thus being the first people to spread the ultimate good news. Remember that the same Church that is accused of being opposed to powerful women was the body that accepted the Gospels as we know them with their emphasis on the Virgin Mary, the dignity of women accused by men of immorality and sin, and their role in believing in Christ being alive when others doubted – all hugely significant and world-changing. Why would this be if Catholicism was opposed to female influence? It is not opposed at all but merely obedient to Christ's teaching about everything. And everything includes never excluding women from the very epicentre of the Church while embracing the exclusively male nature of the priesthood.

Another argument, a favourite today, is that it's just not fair that men can have what women cannot. This is a little like a man complaining that he can't give birth but a woman can, an argument that could be made only by a man who has never stood next to his wife as she delivers their child! Sorry and all that, but men and women are different and gender-bending may work in some areas of life but not in the institution that will take you back to God, the creator of the universe. To loosen and reform the priesthood to include women would be to destroy the priesthood. If you desire a broken cup, you can have it, but the cup is no longer whole or complete and is no longer a cup. Nor is gender the only obstacle as all sorts of men do not qualify for the priesthood, including for the most part those who are married. Or men who are not Catholic, or men who cannot make the sacrifices necessary to be a priest, or men who are considered ill-equipped to be priests. We are all equal in the eyes of God, and baptism gives us the same dignity, but we cannot all be clergy. With regard to influence in the Church, women such as St. Bernadette or Mother Teresa have had a far greater impact and significance than most men and this includes most clergymen, who live glorious but often anonymous lives.

Because of the fashion for claiming sameness in every occupation, there are all sorts of activists who will claim that the Church adopted all-male clergy late in its history and that the early church ordained women. I suppose it would be nice for these zealots if this were the case, but then it would be nice if rainwater were beer and if taxes were paid to us by the government rather than the other way round. Not going to happen. Never did happen. Read the Church fathers, any of the Church fathers, to understand very quickly that priests have always been men and never women. There were certainly women in the early church who belonged to orders of virgins and widows but these were precursors to modern nuns and had nothing to do with early or later priests.

In 1994, Pope John Paul II declared, "Although the teaching that priestly ordination is to be reserved to men alone has been preserved by the constant and universal Tradition of the Church and firmly taught by the Magisterium in its more recent documents, at the present time in some places it is nonetheless considered still open to debate, or the Church's judgment that women are not to be admitted to ordination is considered to have a merely disciplinary force. Wherefore, in order that all doubt may be removed regarding a matter of great importance, a matter which pertains to the Church's divine constitution itself, in virtue of my ministry of confirming the brethren (cf. Luke 22:32), I declare that the Church has no authority whatsoever to confer priestly ordination on women and that this judgment is to be definitively held by all the Church's faithful." The first as well as the last word. The Pope gives us the answer here, and if we refuse to listen to or accept it we can go elsewhere, join another church, and even be ordained in it as a woman minister, a divorced minister, a homosexual minister, or pretty much whatever minister you like. Variety is wonderful but so is Catholicism, and sometimes the two don't mix.

But, runs the argument, even if there is overwhelming evidence that Catholic priests have to be male, surely they can be married and surely this would reduce the number of abuse tragedies. As has already been made clear, abuse occurs within occupations and vocations that do not require celibacy, and abuse also takes place in families and is committed by married men. The issue of married clergy, though, is not as clear cut and absolute as that of male priests. Unlike the dogma of male clergy, which cannot change, this position on marriage is an aspect of canon law and could be altered without denting the truth of the Church. We know, for example, that Peter was married but also that he, and other married men who became priests in the early church, began a new celibate life after ordination. Church fathers in the first four centuries after Christ such as Eusebius, Augustine, Tertullian, Origen, St. Cyril of Jerusalem, and St. Jerome certainly spoke and wrote against married clergy. St. Epiphanius wrote that the "Holy Church respects the dignity of the priesthood to such a point that she does not admit to the diaconate, the priesthood, or the episcopate, nor even to the subdiaconate, anyone still living in marriage and begetting children."[12]

Certainly in Alexandria, Antioch, and Rome, married priests were not the norm, and although married clergy did occur in less urban regions of Christendom, it's important to realize that their behaviour was thought of as being problematic and not approved of. There were virtually no married priests by the third century and this continued for several hundred years. By the ninth century, however, the clergy was in crisis and approaching a state of moral and theological decay. Priests and bishops had begun to marry and have children and were leaving their property – in fact, church property – to their families. There were various attempts in the following century to reform the clergy and restore the former celibacy until in 1139 the Second Lateran Council imposed celibacy on the clergy. The teaching has remained like this ever since.

So the notion that this was some arbitrary and sinister plot by the Church and one that was suddenly imposed on a previously non-celibate church in early medieval Europe is preposterous. Like so many criticisms of Catholicism, it is made by people without any understanding of the actual history of the Church or of dogma. In most circumstances, a belief is codified and confirmed only when it is challenged, the assumption being that it is so self-evident that unless and until challenged it would be redundant to declare it.

Nor is the Church's teaching of priestly celibacy somehow non-Biblical. The Church and the Bible will be discussed in greater length later, but it's crucial to appreciate that the Church is based on the Biblical command that Peter and his descendants will guide and guard Christians and that he and the Magisterium, the teaching office of the Church, will interpret scripture and direct Roman Catholics down the centuries. Christ left us a Pope and a Church and not a Bible. So although the Bible is essential, it is not exclusive in explaining to Christians how they live and believe and cannot be used without the teaching of the Church. In fact, if it is used on its own, it takes away our sense of Christian balance and allows us to fall in all sorts of directions. The Catholic argument becomes perfectly circular and thus plain perfect. Scripture tells us not to be guided by the Bible alone but by the papacy as well as the Bible, thus to believe fully and authentically in the Bible is to be directed by the Pope and the teaching office in their interpretation of the Bible.

The Bible itself does state in Corinthians 7–8 and 32–38 that "it is well for them to remain unmarried as I am. . . . It is well for you to remain as you are. . . . Do not seek a wife. . . . He who refrains from marriage will do better," and Paul writes that celibacy enables us to give "unhindered devotion to the Lord" (1 Cor 7:35). Christ Himself tells us "it is better not to marry. . . . Let anyone accept this who can" (Matt 19:10–12). As with any study of a Biblical text, it's important to understand context. For example, when in Timothy and Titus there appears to be an argument that a bishop or deacon should be "the husband of one wife" what is really being discussed is a man remarrying – it's an attempt to try to remove from the priesthood men who are in a second marriage rather than an argument in favour of married clergy. In early Judaism, the priesthood was maintained within various families and passed down from father to son, thus necessitating marriage. But this is the old covenant, and even within this model priests were required to abstain from having sex with their wives during the time they served in the Temple. Catholics believe that priests fulfil this Temple relationship every day – the Mass and the Eucharist mean they are serving in the Temple every day of their ordained lives.[13]

The Church allows some married priests who convert from Anglicanism to serve as priests in the Catholic Church. Outside of the Latin Rite, there are Catholic priests who are married, but this is the exception to the norm. In the Eastern Rite, where priests are allowed to be married, they have to be married before they are ordained. In other words, if they are celibate at the time of ordination they have to remain so. As well as this, no bishops in the Eastern Rite are allowed to be married.

We sometimes hear that if the Church allowed married priests there would be no crisis in vocations and the seminaries would be full. We could also argue, I suppose, that if we allowed unqualified or semi-believing people to become priests we would also increase the numbers in the seminaries, but lowering the standard, bending the rules, or making them up as we go along hardly seems like good theology and sound morality. In those churches where married priests are allowed, there is a terrible shortage of vocations and any number of other problems. Many of these churches are haemorrhaging members and may cease to exist as genuinely international bodies within half a century or even less. But is there really a vocation problem within the Catholic Church? Not according to the official figures. And, as we've already noted, it's always interesting how, while some friends of the Church do worry about these issues, some of the strongest voices outlining what they see as a vocation catastrophe are those who hope rather than fear that it's a reality. In 1978, for example, there were fewer than 64,000 seminarians internationally whereas the latest figures are closer to 110,000. In the developing world, the increase is even more impressive. Africa has witnessed an increase in vocations to the priesthood of almost 240 per cent and Asia almost 125 per cent. Even in the United States, the numbers are up by close to 60 per cent from thirty years ago. Obviously the numbers in Western Europe and North America are not what they were in the nineteenth century or even the 1950s and before Vatican II and its consequences, but they are increasing and healthy and the quality of seminarians is arguably higher than ever before.

Although married clergy can and do exist in the Church, there are several potential problems and even contradictions. Marriage is a sacrament and is held in extremely high regard but so is the priesthood. A priest must be devoted to his parish and parishioners, and a husband must be devoted to his wife and children. As children and family figure so large – in importance as well as numbers – within Catholicism, a man could well find himself raising several children with his wife while also being required to be constantly available to his flock. It is inevitable that one if not both areas of his life and the lives of those around him would suffer. This seems to be supported by the experience of Protestant ministers, even in some of the most faithful and serious denominations. Focus on the Family is one of the most influential evangelical organizations in the United States if not the world, and according to its research some of the most pressing concerns and problems for married clergy are issues concerning pornography, children, and their sexual relationship with their spouse. Focus's results showed that clergy frequently feel guilty about the lack of time they spend with their families, sometimes leading to depression and family conflict. Within safe, stable societies, all this can be challenging but when it comes to missionary work in what is often a hostile and unstable environment, the situation can be positively dangerous. A priest may put his own life in danger in the mission field but a married minister with children exposes not only himself but those closest to him to the same threats and, tragically, family massacres have occurred several times.

I'm fully aware that for some people the very fact that I have tried to put the abuse horror in context, explain what happened, and give the reasons why the priesthood is as it is will make no difference to their anger, but I also know that to some critics any response from a Catholic apart from blanket criticism of the Church is considered inadequate. It is always stunning and humbling to hear that many of the actual victims do not think in this way at all, and the harshest words about the Church generally come from observers. For those who are defined by their dislike of all things Catholic, there is little that can be said. For the victims, many of them still wonderful Catholics in spite of what they have suffered, we can only offer our sorrow, prayers, and solidarity. It's horrific to consider it but there will doubtless be future and further cases of abuse that come to light. Some in the media and public life will take a sordid delight in drawing any number of conclusions based on their own prejudices and fantasies as opposed to the genuine facts. Today the Roman Catholic Church is one of the safest places for a young person to be. The Church has learned from its failings and has worked and is still working to deal with the pain caused by those who abused vulnerable and innocent adolescents and thus abused the Church as well. For some of the abused, the wounds will never heal, and for that every Catholic must feel shame and regret. The whole saga is a condemnation of abuse, immorality, and exploitation but not a condemnation of the Church. It is the Church that insists that there is a right and wrong and the world that tries to blur the line.

CATHOLICS AND HISTORY

THE ROMAN CATHOLIC CHURCH, we are repeatedly told, has over the course of history been like some enormous, theological, and social evil shadow or ghost that haunts and frightens otherwise progressive and enlightened peoples. From serious historians to television comedy shows, it is the Church that frequently gets the blame. Actually the Church has generally been ethically and politically ahead of its time and throughout history has been an enlightened and enlightening force. Even so, the institution itself and certainly some people within the institution have not always acted in the best manner and have failed the Church. But seldom has the Roman Catholic Church been the dark knight, or the dark night, that its critics so often claim. The reason this subject requires an entire chapter and comes so early in the book is that most of the time the attacks on Catholicism are based on either a misunderstanding or deliberate misinterpretation of history. No need to bother with complex issues of theology and morality when one can merely condemn the Church for its role in the Crusades, the Inquisition, the persecution of Galileo and resistance to science, the Holocaust, and any other event that appears to put Catholicism on the defensive. It's part of the digression approach – rather than get to the genuine arguments we'll try to head you off at the pass or, if you like, there is no way I'm going to talk about the truth of Catholic arguments when I can use popular ignorance and prejudice to imply that the Church has to be wrong now because it was always on the wrong side of history. Even if it had been so, and it most certainly hasn't, this would indicate very little about its claims being either true or false.

The litany of attacks is tired, dull, and misplaced, and it's sometimes tempting to give in and just agree that Catholic history is awful but we're really very sorry, intend to learn from our mistakes, and don't worry too much because everything changed after Vatican II and it won't happen again. Honestly. Peace, love, hugs, and aching revisionism all round and then some meaningful guitar-playing. Problem is, apart from being untrue and intellectually tragic, it's also just plain meagre and silly and doesn't deal with the facts. The notion held by some Catholics today that the Church in the past was always wrong only encourages critics and, frankly, who can blame them? It's nonsense, of course, but generally used as an excuse by passive Catholics who would rather avoid an argument than defend their Church. Of course Catholics sometimes acted appallingly and of course the Church sometimes acted in spite of rather than because of Catholicism but it would be astounding if that were not the case. There's something important here. Evil committed in the name of Christ and His Church can never be truly Christian and Catholic because Christ never taught evil, unlike other creeds and faiths where founders have indeed preached violence, slaughter, intolerance, and hatred. While acknowledging wrongs, we are obliged by truth and common sense to point out what really happened and to ask why those people with a moral code that they make up as they go along and who do not believe in God or right and wrong have such a problem with nastiness in the first place. Or to put it another way, what gives them the absolutes by which to judge other people?

History matters. We learn from it and we're shaped by it, but sometimes we do tend to repeat its mistakes. If what happened in the past was irrelevant, the past would not be used to attack the Church in the way it so often is. Think of history as a series of stones in a flowing river. We step from one to the other and then safely reach the other side. Ignore the stones or try to rush across too quickly from first to second and to third and we sink or drown. The stones are there not to be stood on for too long – this produces monomaniacs and eccentric traditionalists – but if we pretend that they do not exist we do so at our peril. History matters.

Long, long ago in a country far, far away, armies of brutish, greedy, and stupid men with crosses on their chests invaded a peaceful and tolerant land and tried to convert people to Christianity – when, that is, not slaughtering innocent boys and girls or refusing to learn to read and write or, perish the thought, take a simple bath once in a while. Thus the Crusades. Catholics bad, Muslims good. It tends to be the first attack we hear because of a whole club of issues: the rise of Islamic radicalism, the crisis in the Middle East, and the fact that Muslim extremists who know even less about history than Western anti-Catholics label everyone who isn't Muslim and who lives in Europe and North America as Crusaders. It's painted in mass-market fiction, in much of even credible media, and in many lecture halls and classrooms as a time when the Pope revealed Catholicism to be truly animalistic and violent. It was that great moral theologian and medieval historian Kevin Costner in the movie *Robin Hood, Prince of Thieves* who explained that his father, Robin Hood senior, was opposed to the Crusades because he thought it foolish and wrong to try to convert others to your own religion. Robin and his pals then spent much of the rest of the movie showing Catholic monks as drunken clowns, Catholic bishops as corrupt fatties, and Muslim warriors as the only modern, sensible people around. Robin's dad may have had the right idea but he was a little dim if he actually thought that forced conversion was what the Crusades were all about – forced conversion was expressly forbidden by the Church and there was hardly any concerted attempt to convert Muslims in the Holy Land, Christians were always in a minority, and the Crusaders assumed that this would always be the case and never tried to make it otherwise. However, if as Christians we believe that we have found the key to salvation and happiness and then refuse to tell others about it, we really are selfish and cruel. Neither Robin nor Robin's dad, of course, has the final word on early medieval geopolitics and religious conflict, but this and so many other movies, television shows, and novels stress an absurdity that has become common belief: that what is now Israel, Palestine, Syria, Lebanon, Jordan, and the surrounding area was somehow content, peaceful, and righteous before and until European knights invaded and did what, we are also told, European knights always did – raped, pillaged, destroyed, murdered, and so on.

As we will see, the Crusades was never imperialism as we know it in any modern form; the region had been strongly Christian long before it was conquered by Islamic cavalry; Christendom was provoked over and over again by vehement and highly aggressive Muslim expansion; the Crusades were barely acknowledged in the Islamic world until the late nineteenth century because the Muslims thought them largely irrelevant; cruelty did occur but was nowhere near as common or extreme as usually suggested; and Islam was rarely as tolerant and pluralistic as its apologists both within and outside its religion and culture now claim.

First we need to establish what the Crusades were and when they happened. They began in 1095 when Pope Urban II made a preaching tour through France; what we know as the First Crusade took place between 1096 and 1102, with the capture of Jerusalem happening in the summer of 1099. Because Jerusalem needed support from neighbouring areas, other Christian settlements were established in Antioch, Tripoli, and Edessa, and all of these were aided by military intervention throughout the first half of the twelfth century, with the Second Crusade taking place between 1147 and 1149. Crusades were not, however, confined to the Holy Land in this period; they also took place in Spain, Germany, the Baltic, Poland, Bohemia, and even against enemies of the papacy in Italy, but these do have the popular resonance and are not clouded in the same mythology and fallacy as the struggles in Palestine, for all sorts of modern political, emotional, and theological reasons.[1]

Jerusalem and most of the region fell to the Muslim leader Saladin in 1187. Although the Third Crusade (1189–92) and the German Crusade (1197–98) recaptured much that was lost, the city of Jerusalem remained in Islamic hands. There were popular and largely non-military expeditions in 1212 (the Children's Crusade) and 1251 (the Crusade of the Shepherds), and then military campaigns with the Fourth Crusade (1202–1204), which was diverted to Constantinople, and the Fifth Crusade (1217–29), which resulted in the temporary recapture of Jerusalem until it was lost again in 1244. The Fifth Crusade captured Jerusalem, but the Muslims had destroyed the walls before the arrival of the Crusader Army, so the Christians were unable to hold it once the Crusader army returned to Europe. Frederick II, the Holy Roman Emperor, led the Sixth Crusade. He made a treaty with the Muslims in 1229 whereby Jerusalem would be handed over to the Christians. The treaty lasted ten years, and in 1244 Jerusalem was once again conquered by the Muslims. Other Crusader campaigns were launched by the French in the 1260s and 1280s, and Crusader armies also entered Egypt and Tunisia at various times in the thirteenth century. In 1309 and 1320, there were further Crusades and numerous smaller campaigns in the eastern Mediterranean. Crusading continued in different forms and sometimes as crusading leagues right up until the sixteenth century – including the great victory at Lepanto in 1571 – and the wars in the late seventeenth century to recover large parts of the Balkans from the Turks.[2]

These were most certainly not colonial wars, and anybody who assumes that they were some sort of early Western imperialism clearly has no idea about either the Crusades or about Western, or for that matter Eastern, imperialism. The purpose of empire is to make money and extend power by controlling the economy and resources of a foreign country and culture, by exploiting its people and increasing the influence of the imperial power. The Crusades were not profitable for the Crusaders and actually bankrupted many noble families due to the enormous cost of arming a knight and his retinue and maintaining them in a land so far away from France, England, or Germany. If financial gain was the intention, there were far easier pickings in Europe or even within a home country, what with profit from a ransom of an enemy or the capture of fertile land. There was hardly any attempt during the campaigns to use the local economy to enrich Europe, and the Muslim population tended to continue its financial, working, and business life as it had done before, often in fact making more money due to the need on the part of the European population for supplies. Just as there was no serious, concerted attempt to convert Muslims to Christianity, there was no serious attempt to use them as an imperial workforce. A few historians and far more uninformed commentators have claimed that Crusaders were the sons of poor aristocratic families desperately in need of cash who were sent to the Holy Land for plunder and that these men, often the clan failures, tended to be more violent and unscrupulous than even their brothers back home. There was never very much evidence to support this claim, and modern scholarship shows the contrary – the knights were often the cream of European chivalric society and their loss devastated their host nations.[3]

A more difficult question than when they occurred is what the Crusades actually were. At heart they were wars of penitence, armed pilgrimages by Christians fighting for a specifically Christian cause – to regain Christian holy places, Christian shrines, and once-Christian states and to liberate and protect Christian people. All done with the certain knowledge that what they were doing was holy and just and was the right thing to do. The Crusades seemed to fulfil the demands of a just war, which was and is based on three fundamentals: the first being as a response to unjustified aggression, the second being a war on the orders of a legitimate government or authority, and the third being a conflict undertaken with the right intentions and with moral behaviour in the course of that war. What they were not were the caricatures of modern imagination, which arose as late as the nineteenth century in two rather different works of literature – Sir Walter Scott's 1825 novel *The Talisman* and Joseph Francois Michaud's *History of the Crusades*, published in six volumes between 1812 and 1822.

Scott's historical novels were almost all a mingling of romance and fantasy with, at best, only one foot tenuously placed in genuine historical understanding. Sometimes the man lost his balance completely! There's nothing wrong with that as long as they are read for fun, as picturesque period pieces and little if anything more. The problem with *The Talisman* – a story of a Scottish knight on the Third Crusade, of his lady love, of Saladin as a noble soul who actually cures Richard the Lion Hearted, and of brave but vulgar and primitive Crusaders battling far more urban and enlightened Muslims – was not that it was horribly inaccurate but that it was devoured by one of the most credulous and unstable rulers in early twentieth-century Europe. Kaiser Wilhelm II of Germany was raised on Scott by his English mother and took historical romances far more seriously than was altogether appropriate. Then again, he was a bit of a clown, but a clown in charge of the most powerful army in the world. When he visited Damascus in 1898, he made an absurdly grand, Wagneresque pilgrimage to Saladin's tomb, thus leading some of the most influential Muslims to wonder why they, rather than a Christian monarch from Europe, had not fully realized Saladin's greatness. It's difficult to believe it after the century of revisionism and mythology around Saladin that has so lionized the man, but from his death until the early 1900s he had been largely forgotten by the Islamic world.[4]

Michaud's massive and massively flawed history took an entirely different approach from that of the novelist Scott. Michaud was a French nationalist and royalist who studied and understood the Crusades through the prism of the recent and contemporary French experience. The French, he wrote, had not only led the Crusades but had benefited from them and were duty-bound to continue the spirit of their medieval adventure throughout history. It was the nation's destiny, he said. Part of his analysis was entirely accurate but he mistakenly believed, and stressed, that the Crusades were a pursuit of empire and that France should still be an imperial power and increase the size and scope of its empire – a Gallic place in the sun. This was not only extraordinarily anachronistic but it was dreadful history and encouraged the French and a French empire in South-East Africa, North Africa, and the Middle East in a way that the Crusaders would never have understood. Encouraged by the French model, other European states looked to their crusading past, and nationalists in Scandinavia, Germany, and England also adopted the atavistic crusading memory, many of them assuming that every European intervention abroad was somehow in the direct tradition of medieval knights. They never were.

This twisting of history by Europeans inevitably began to bleed into the Muslim understanding of the Crusades. It was an understanding that, contrary to what we think today, had little or no historical significance. Since the 1980s in particular, we have heard Islamic extremists and even some relative moderates speak of "Crusaders" when they describe Western governments and their armies, and this implies a long-established Muslim perception of Christendom and its secular successors. Not so. Until the end of the nineteenth century, the Crusades had been largely forgotten and when they were considered, it was in the context of a great Islamic triumph over the forces of alien Christianity. Rather than assuming themselves to be victims and weak, Muslims viewed the Crusades through the image of victory and strength. All this changed in the 1890s as the Turkish Ottoman Empire, the sick man of Europe who refused to consult a doctor, was disintegrating under economic decline, nationalist resentment and rebellion, and an archaic rule that had not kept pace with the new idea of western Europe and North America. The Turkish leader Sultan Abdulhamid II quite cynically embraced Pan-Islamism and offered himself as the leader of a new caliphate to unite the entire Muslim world. The idea required an enemy and what better than the notion that the Europe that was infringing on the Ottoman Empire was dedicated to some new crusade as a replica of the medieval original. The European powers that were threatening the sultan's empire, of course, had little concern for religion and had abandoned Christians several times in the century when a Turkish alliance was in their interests – Britain and France, for example, had joined with Turkey against Russia during the Crimean War. The new conflict between Europe and the Ottoman Empire and the Turkish decline were far more about geopolitics, power, money, and trading than it was about messiahs and prophets.

But this new language of victimhood found an eager audience in the Islamic world, particularly after the publication in 1899 of the first history of the Crusades by a Muslim scholar, Sayyid 'Ali al-Hariri. At the same time, young Arabs, Christian (often Arab nationalists) as well as Muslim, were travelling to Europe for an education and learning from their liberal European colleagues who had embraced the fashionable views of the Crusades that the Muslims had been wronged and oppressed. When the British defeated the Turks during the First World War and, with their French allies, occupied entire regions of the Middle East, the paranoia about the new Crusade seemed to be confirmed. That the Jewish presence in Palestine was increasing, to be transformed into an official state in 1948, only added to the fantasy. Today the narrative of the Muslim world sees communism, Zionism, and even atheism as all part of some strange package that represents a crusading renaissance. What the Christians failed to achieve a thousand years ago, many argue, they now try to accomplish through other and sometimes the same means.

The entire thesis is absurd on any number of levels but the Western world is too timid in its self-identity and confidence and too bathed in political correctness to aggressively contradict the argument. More than this, self-styled Western intellectuals and journalists seem to confirm Islamic fears, misusing the word *Crusades* and having even less understanding of and just as much hatred for Christianity and Christian history as the shapers of Muslim opinion. There is some excuse for the Muslim attitude, little for the Western one. The general view in the West in particular is that the Crusades were so wrong that even the Pope – obviously not a particularly good man in the eyes of some of the fiercest critics of Catholic history because he leads the Catholic Church – apologized for them. Actually he didn't. On the first Sunday of Lent in the year 2000, Pope John Paul II led a day of pardon and repentance in which he asked "forgiveness from the Lord for the sins, past and present, of the sons and daughters of the Church." The Crusades were not mentioned but a statement was made concerning contrition for "sins committed in the service of truth." The papacy did apologize to the Orthodox Church for the 1204 sack of Constantinople – of which we'll learn more later – which was an entirely correct thing to do. The truth, however, is that most critics of Catholicism who try to use the Crusades as a battering ram are as condemning of Eastern Orthodoxy as they are of Roman Catholicism, don't even know about what happened in 1204, and would much rather expose supposed anti-Muslim behaviour than internecine Christian injustice. In other words, the real papal apology to the Orthodox faith is not as important to them as the alleged apology he made to Islam.

The Crusades were a response to a plea from the terrified population of the Christian lands of the east, mostly Eastern

Orthodox, whose cities and countries were being invaded by the Seljuk Turks. This Islamic expansion was nothing new and had begun almost as early as Islam itself. The Middle East, North Africa, the Levant, and the neighbouring and surrounding areas were by the fifth century heavily Christian, with many of the Church fathers and leaders of the Church coming from and living in the region.[5] There were Christian and pagan minorities but, obviously, no Muslims because Mohammad was not even born until around the year 570. Yet as early as 638, Islamic armies had conquered Jerusalem and had gone on to occupy most of North Africa by the end of the century. They had conquered Spain by 711, and it was only the victory of Charles Martel at Tours and Poitier in 732 that halted what was then seen as the seemingly unstoppable Muslim domination of Europe. The centre of eastern Christianity in Constantinople retained parts of its empire but had lost Palestine, Syria, and North Africa and hundreds of thousands of Christians to war, execution, and forced conversion.

There were naturally a number of Christians, Jews, and others who voluntarily embraced Islam, but the image of an entire non-Muslim world suddenly pleading to become Muslim is frankly absurd. Conversion and cultural and theological shift were largely the results of military dominance, and change of religion took place out of fear and a disappointing but understandable desire to become part of the clearly ascendant group within the area. Enormous numbers of Christians refused to become Muslim and experienced varying degrees of tolerance and oppression in the new Islamic empire – at best their state of dhimmitude, a protected but controlled usually Christian or Jewish minority within an Islamic state – gave them relative security but kept them in a humiliating condition in which they were second-class citizens required to pay a special tax and to be subservient to their Muslim compatriots and restricted in how they could maintain churches and conduct their religious life. There seems to be a campaign today to portray Islamic countries in the medieval age as islands of pluralism and coexistence in an otherwise cruel, intolerant, and Christian ocean. Although it's certainly true that European Christians sometimes betrayed the primary text of their faith and the founding values of the Church in the way they treated minorities, they were certainly no worse than their Islamic rivals. The Muslim conquest and conversion of the Middle East and central and southern Asia is unparalleled in its military precision, speed, and determination.[6]

By the eleventh century, the Arab empire had divided into three separate areas of rule, based in Spain, Egypt, and Iraq and Persia. The Fatimid dynasty in Egypt had control of Jerusalem, and by 1027 Constantinople had managed to secure various rights and privileges from Egypt for the Christians of the city most sacred to Christianity – Jerusalem is only the third-holiest place in Islam – and guaranteed the safety of pilgrims from Europe who made the always dangerous journey to the city. This changed with the coming of the Seljuk Turks, who first took Christian Armenia and then all of Anatolia, defeating the armies of eastern Christianity in 1071 at the battle of Manzikert. The emperor Alexios Komnenos took over a decaying eastern empire and managed to halt the decline, partly by coming to terms with a papacy that had previously been viewed with deep suspicion by Orthodox Christians. This new relationship led directly to an armed intervention by Catholic Europe when the persecution of Christians and attacks on Christian pilgrims became unbearable. Thus began the Crusades. They were a response to the Islamic conquest of Christian lands and Christian peoples; in many ways it is remarkable that Christian armies did not take action sooner. Today we are incredulous that this should have happened; it says a great deal about the time and the fact that the Crusades did not come as a surprise to the Muslims, who intended to take all of Christian Europe as well as the Christian east and would try to do so for centuries to come. They had expected a Christian response for decades.[7]

†

Were the Crusades brutal, were they justified by Christian thought, were they unique in the medieval world? They certainly were brutal, in that warfare and battle were brutal in the Middle Ages, but then military clashes are seldom peaceful and loving and are not supposed to be. War is bloody, nasty, and brutish, and never more so than in the great atheistic twentieth century when God-hating and religion-hating military dictators such as Hitler and Stalin murdered tens of millions. The entire idea of mass civilian casualties is very much a post-enlightenment way of thinking that did not exist in the Christian world. It was the French Revolution and the cult of the godless that introduced mass citizen armies and mass citizen slaughter. But the Crusades were certainly of the time. Cities that refused to surrender were usually sacked, and enemies who fought on after quarter was offered were often killed. The Crusaders treated their Muslim enemies as they treated their Christian enemies at home in Europe and exactly how they expected to be treated – and were – by their Muslim enemies in the Middle East.[8]

Whether the Crusades and the Crusaders were justified by Christianity is a more difficult and challenging question. Christ was a man of peace and the prince of peace, but He was not a pacifist. He took a heavy whip to men who were shaming the Temple, advised His followers to arm themselves while on the road, and when speaking to a Roman soldier about God and faith never insisted that the man leave his position in one of the most aggressive and imperialistic armies in history. To turn one's cheek when attacked is fundamentally different from abandoning another person to a violent assault, let alone an entire people to oppression. Some exegetes see the deliberate turning of the specified cheek as an act of resistance to any attempt to dismiss or ignore the dignity of the one being struck, an act not of "pacifism" but of "protest."

Remember, the Pope finally responded to pleas from the eastern Christian empire after years of persecution and violence. Pope Innocent III wrote, "How does a man love according to divine precept his neighbour as himself when, knowing that his Christian brothers in faith and in name are held by the perfidious Muslims in strict confinement and weighed down by the yoke of heaviest servitude, he does not devote himself to the task of freeing them? . . . Is it by chance that you do not know that many thousands of Christians are bound in slavery and imprisoned by the Muslims, tortured with innumerable torments?"

Compared to those who took part in internal European wars and in conflicts that have occurred since the Crusades, the men who undertook these campaigns do not stand out as being better or worse than any other soldier in battle. Yet because of the explicitly Christian nature of the phenomenon, a whole cloud of disdain has developed, often built mostly on mythology and what critics like to think happened. One common attack is that the Crusaders not only fought with Muslim armies but massacred innocent Jews whenever they had the opportunity.

As usual when discussing Christian history, there is some truth in this accusation but a heavy dose of nonsense as well.

Anti-Jewish riots certainly did occur in parts of the Rhineland but were isolated and never initiated by the Church, the leadership of which did all it could to protect the Jewish community. Shortly before the First Crusade, bands of peasants, mostly illiterate and drunk on the idea of a holy war, planned to march to the east to fight Muslims and long before they had left even their own local state began to attack the Jews. In Speyer, the bishop heroically protected the Jewish population, at great risk to his life. At Worms, the bishop hid and housed Jews in his own home, but the armed peasants smashed their way in and killed every Jewish man, woman, and child they could find. Similarly at Mainz and in a number of towns on the road to Cologne, this same mob attacked Jews and those communities were protected, with varying degrees of success, by the Catholic bishops and clergy. In Trier, for example, the archbishop brought the local Jewish population into his palace and almost all of them were saved. During the Second Crusade, St. Bernard of Clairvaux made the journey to the Rhineland to personally demand an end to any anti-Semitic violence and physically prevented further violence. He told his fellow Catholics, "Ask anyone who knows the Sacred Scriptures what he finds foretold of the Jews in the Psalm. 'Not for their destruction do I pray,' it says. The Jews are for us the living words of Scripture, for they remind us always of what our Lord suffered. . . . Under Christian princes they endure a hard captivity, but 'they only wait for the time of their deliverance.'" Hardly the mythology of a crazed Catholic Church telling its followers to murder Jews as a precursor to the mass slaughter of Muslims.[9]

The attack on Constantinople has not led to Catholic-Jewish

tension but caused a bitter division between the Catholic and Orthodox Church for several centuries. Innocent III had been elected Pope in 1198 and was committed to reclaiming the Holy Land, which had been lost to Saladin. French Crusaders had been told to sail directly to Palestine from Venice, but the army's numbers were smaller than anticipated by the Venetians, who had collected a large fleet and wanted to be paid for the ships whether they were used or not. Desperate for money, the Crusaders were told that if they conquered the Dalmatian city of Zara, then in rebellion, they would be able to pay the Venetians. Zara, however, was not only Catholic but was ruled by a king who was also a Crusader, and the Pope promptly excommunicated the French knights who attacked the city. In time these men were accepted back into the Church but still owed money to the Venetian bankers who had purchased the fleet. Alexios, the exiled son of the deposed Byzantine emperor, realized that he could use the unstable situation and a well-armed Crusader army for his own purposes. He wanted to take back the throne. If the Crusaders helped him take Constantinople, he told them, he would not only pay off the Venetians but provide the Crusaders with the ships and supplies to sail for Palestine. When the Pope heard of this, he ordered the Crusaders – who had already disobeyed him over Zara – to ignore Alexios, have nothing to do with Constantinople, and move immediately to the Holy Land.

Tragically, but perhaps predictably, it was not to be the case. In June 1203, the French Crusaders and their Venetian allies arrived at the gates of Constantinople and Alexios was placed back on the throne with his father. Early the following year, however, Alexios was murdered when the people of Constantinople rose up against his rule, and the Crusaders, already disappointed by the meagre amounts in the government treasury and Alexios's inability to properly compensate them, stormed the sacred epicentre of Christian Orthodoxy and killed, raped, stole, and destroyed. It was a despicable and disgraceful episode, impossible to justify or excuse. But it doesn't say very much at all about the papacy or the Church. Pope Innocent had pleaded with these particular Crusaders to leave Constantinople alone, and there is no evidence that he at any time sent mixed or misleading messages or did anything other than demand that this army do what it had been assembled to do and attempt to liberate the pontiff's beloved Jerusalem. It has also been suggested that this was all part of some elaborate ploy to bring Constantinople and the eastern empire into the Roman Catholic world and under papal authority. It's a conspiracy theory run wild. The Pope was far more concerned with Palestine than Constantinople, and this atrocity made any hope of Jerusalem's recapture extraordinarily difficult. The worst thing that can be said about the Pope's involvement and actions is that while Innocent III was one of the strongest popes in the history of the papacy, thirteenth-century communications were not very advanced, so once the crusading army left Italy there was no way for anyone, even a pope as powerful as Innocent III, to control events. Brutes acted as brutes, Catholics did not act as Catholics.

The taking of Jerusalem in 1099 has also been depicted as a uniquely shocking moral and literal bloodbath – men walking knee-deep in gore and thousands of bodies torn apart in the streets in the city where Christ walked. The great success of the Crusades, the capture of Jerusalem, the story runs, also reflected the inherent violence of the Crusaders and their cause. As usual, history is not usually quite as clear and polarized between good and bad as that. The Crusaders were deeply spiritual and religious people, but today we might interpret some of that religiosity as superstition and credulity – they were convinced that when they finally reached Jerusalem having fought so many fierce and costly battles, the city and the Holy Sepulchre within it would be given to them by God without any resistance. In fact, the Fatimids had won Jerusalem back from the Turks a year earlier, and these Muslims, as opposed to the Turks, would almost certainly have come to an agreement with the Crusaders to allow Christian access to holy places and sites of pilgrimage, as they had done in the past. Be that as it may, the latest rulers of the city refused to surrender when the Crusaders arrived and adopted the standard defensive positions of a besieged force. There were days of prayer and fasting from the Christian armies and even a heavily mocked barefoot march around Jerusalem in the hope that such a gesture would please God and lead the walls of the city to collapse. Lack of shoes failed but the presence of siege towers, catapults, and a massive battering ram was far more effective. The Crusaders broke through on July 15, 1099.

What happened next does not make for comfortable reading and the same applies to any account of a taken city in the medieval period. Many defenders were killed. Muslims who took shelter in the al-Aqsa mosque, as well as Jews who barricaded themselves into a synagogue, were slaughtered. As repugnant as this was, they were combatants who had been trying to kill Crusaders just an hour before – there were Jewish soldiers allied to the Muslim forces in the defence of Jerusalem. The Christian soldiers were out of control, which was again a frequent occurrence in sieges in the Middle Ages: the combination of relief after constant fear of death, the desire for revenge on those who had killed friends and colleagues, the lust for food and water, the unleashing of the basest of animal instincts that exist within man. The actions were not organized and we know from Hebrew sources found in Cairo that Jewish prisoners were taken to Ashkelon, where they were ransomed by Egyptian Jews who had heard of their capture. The same sources also record the respect shown toward women – Jewish and Muslim – by the Crusaders and notes that this was not typical of other battles that had taken place in the Holy Land. We also know that wholesale massacre could not have occurred because as well as the ransoming of prisoners a number of Muslims were expelled – a source as unsympathetic as Saladin himself proves this because he discovered the descendants of the Jerusalem garrison in Damascus, where their parents had fled after being removed by the Crusaders and sent to Syria. Expulsions of people thought to be dangerous and opposed to the government were, again, typical if not desirable. Christians, for example, had been systematically purged from the city by the Fatimids before the Crusaders arrived. Prisoners, however, were certainly killed and so were some women and children; even if this was out of fear because an Arab army was in the region and the Christians were frightened of leaving Jerusalem with a small guard and a large Muslim population, it still does not justify the killing of the defeated.[10]

So what are we to conclude about the Crusades? They were not the proudest moment of Christian history but nor were they the childish caricature of modern Western guilt and certainly not that of contemporary Muslim paranoia. Most Catholics feel shame about what happened and apologize for wrongs that occurred, but it is almost unheard of to hear Islamic leaders offering any form of contrition for the Islamic conquest of the Christian heartlands of the Middle East. The impulse generally does not exist in a Muslim people told by their scholars that the Crusades were uniquely evil and anti-Muslim, especially when this attitude is enabled or empowered by Western anti-Christians. Indeed, it is not uncommon in radical Islamic circles today to hear of calls for a reconquest of Spain, let alone the establishment of a Muslim theocracy in the entire Middle East.

The attack on Catholic history usually begins with the Crusades, but nobody expects the Spanish Inquisition. Actually, everybody expects the Spanish Inquisition. Not that they mean the Spanish Inquisition specifically, but rather the graphic image of sneering prelates and lascivious priests and monks torturing noble folk who dared to question some esoteric or absurd lump of Catholic teaching. Once again the underlying premise is that Catholics are somehow nastier than anyone else – only the Church could organize something like the Inquisition, which was unnecessary, was horribly cruel, and is entirely typical of the intolerance and desire for violence inherent within Roman Catholicism. That belief might be convenient but it's also ridiculous. Remember that Spain was a superpower in the sixteenth century, and its enemies produced copious amounts of propaganda as one of the few ways that they could challenge the influence of the Spanish state. The numbers of people hurt or even affected by the Spanish Inquisition have been vastly exaggerated – more babies are killed in abortions every two days in North America alone than people died in the entire Inquisition. Or to use another comparison, more men and women were slaughtered in a couple of weeks of the terror of the atheistic French Revolution than in a century of the Inquisition. Even taking into account the hideous advances in mass-murder techniques of the twentieth century, the countless victims of the barbaric and aggressively God-hating regimes of Hitler, Stalin, Mau, or

Pol Pot make deaths at the hands of the Inquisition seem almost trivial. But death and injustice are never matters of trivia.

Yet even less odious comparisons are revealing. The Inquisition did not hold people without trial or even charges, as occurs today in Guantanamo Bay, for example; nor did it refuse to provide a legal defence for the accused, as occurs today in human rights bodies in civilized and secular countries such as Canada. There are examples of common criminals purposely blaspheming because they preferred the justice of the Inquisition to that of the secular courts, and most of those who appeared before the Inquisition were found innocent and sent on their way; many others who were found to have contravened church teaching were asked to recant or reform and it was unusual for violence and execution to occur. There were also inquisitions in a number of Protestant nations, sometimes far more thorough and brutal in their oppression, particularly of those suspected of witchcraft. Even the Victorian Protestant historian Henry Charles Lea, who spent much of his life studying and writing about the Inquisition and was no friend of the Catholic Church, conceded that the victims of the Inquisition were "relatively few" and that at times the Inquisition was all that stood between civilization and moral anarchy.[11] Historian Warren H. Carroll puts matters well in his multi-volume history of the Christian story: "But in fact the heretic in Christendom was in every sense of the word a revolutionary, as dangerous to public order and personal safety as yesterday's Communist or today's terrorist. They brought fear, cruelty, bloodshed, and war wherever they appeared in sufficient numbers."[12] But the Inquisition did exist and did do wrong, and from this we cannot and must not hide.

The history and origins of the Inquisition are less sinister and more straightforward than we might think. The Church has always tried to prevent or respond to errors within the faith – there is the persistent idea today that Christianity consists of people merely being nice to each other and only getting a little cross, and not about the cross, and then being sorry about it, if things become particularly difficult. Turning the other cheek has been transformed into indifference to wrong and the story of the woman caught in adultery and Christ's teaching against hypocrisy transformed into a scolding against anyone who has an opinion that's insufficiently progressive or permissive. Christianity is about salvation and a moral code and belief system that leads to that salvation. The Church exists to save souls, not to make people feel good about themselves. Therefore it's vital to defend the truth and defend the Church that preserves it. From the earliest days of Christianity, the founding Christians chastised, suspended, or even expelled people from the community if they refused to amend their ways and if they rejected church teaching. Heresy was not invented in the sixteenth century and has always been seen in religious societies as something deadly not only to individual believers but to the entire world around them that they might be influenced and infected by such errors. Pagan Rome had its form of inquisition where those considered heretics, including Christians, were challenged and sometimes executed. To a certain extent, the Church followed these precedents, which in some ways explains but in no way forgives what happened. The papacy certainly understands this, and Pope John Paul II made it completely clear when he said of the various historical failings including the Inquisition, "We are asking pardon for the divisions among Christians . . . and for attitudes of mistrust and hostility assumed toward followers of other religions."[13]

Part of the problem of any discussion of the issue is that it's difficult today for people to appreciate the connection between church and state in the medieval and early modern world. Citizenship assumed religious uniformity and anyone who wasn't part of the state faith – be it Islam in the Muslim world or Anglicanism in England, for example – would be treated with suspicion at the very least. This blurred and complicated the Christian ideal, the expansion of which was supposed to be based on an attempt to convert by argument and example and never by force. Christians sometimes failed in this, but it has never been Catholic teaching to bring people into the Church with violence and pressure, and the Inquisition was supposed only to have power over baptized Christians.

The Inquisition as such was not some single, permanent body but a multi-dimensional institution that did different things and behaved in different ways depending on when and where it operated. Inquisitions were local. There were inquisitions all over the Catholic world, but in many areas they were almost entirely inactive; in Germany, the Inquisition was generally passive and in England remained quiet for decades on end. The Inquisitions were asked to intervene in cases of heresy and for centuries heresy was rare. This all changed in the twelfth and thirteenth centuries with the Albigensian or Cathar movement, particularly in the south of France. Today it's become fashionable to see the Albigensians as reformers who were trying to restore the purity and simplicity of Christianity or good people who were ahead of their time and rejected the bellicose God of the Old Testament. The God of the Old Testament is the God of the New, but more to the point these zealots were hardly peace-loving premature hippies – in 1208 they murdered the representative of Pope Innocent III and promised the same for any further delegates from the Church. They believed that the material world and the human body were created by Satan and thus were evil; they were vehemently opposed to marriage, family, and childbearing. They also denied the validity of oaths, which formed the very basis of feudal society. They had a strict sense of hierarchy, with a self-appointed elite controlling the ordinary members and often using them for their own pleasures. In many ways, they were comparable to a modern cult. They were in most respects a rival or alternative religion to Catholicism and cloaked themselves in a Christian context and tried to convert people away from the Church.[14]

Initially the Church tried to argue the Cathars out of their ideas, and for some years the Dominicans in particular preached and wrote in an attempt to put matters right and engineer reconciliation. But this attempt failed, and a crusade was called by the Pope, emphasizing that the Cathars had to be educated, their confessions heard, and their route back into Christianity made as easy and fluid as possible. That hope did not materialize. The Cathars had become deeply unpopular in the regions where they operated, and over two decades they were attacked by peasant mobs, armies, and local religious and military leaders. The Cathars were destroyed, but the Church realized that this was no way to deal with militant heresy. As tempting as it is for critics to assume the papacy wanted the Inquisition to exist so as to maximize brutality, it actually established it to minimize the anarchy and violence that had occurred in France.

In 1231, Pope Gregory ordered the Dominicans to take charge of papal courts and decisions and so prevent mob rule and guarantee that the accused received a fair trial and the right of defence. This was the foundation of the Inquisition, and it was a move to organize, control, and limit violence, disruption, and division. Of course, it often failed and even achieved the opposite of its stated and original purpose, but it's surprising how often in an age of casual and brutal violence a relative moderation and legality was achieved. Civil law was far harsher than canon law, demanding confiscation of a heretic's property and usually death, something the Church had tried to prevent for generations. In place of this, the Inquisition functioned like modern circuit courts, going into a particular area to deal not with criminal and civil but religious law. The Inquisition would have priests preach and teach and then remain in a town or village for a period of time to hear confession and advise people on spiritual direction and appropriate repentance. This was a grace period and was strictly observed. If, however, at the end of it those suspected of heresy still refused to admit their errors and to reform, they were tried and, if found guilty, were excommunicated and handed over to secular judges for sentencing.

It's important to grasp that while the popular imagination has the Inquisition determined to maim and kill, the central aim was actually to bring people back to the Church. A soul saved was a success, a person executed was a failure. Even if we cynically apply selfish motives to everybody involved, this would not have led to gratuitous violence but an obsessive effort to remove the heresy from the person rather than the person from the world. Although no priest, monk, or member of any religious order was allowed to use torture, the Inquisition did use torture and people did suffer terribly, as they did when tortured by state bodies, the police and militia, the military, Islamic societies, and virtually every other power and force in medieval society. Torture existed. It was used. Often. The Inquisition used it no more and usually less than other authorities with judicial power in the era – entire pamphlets were written on the limits of torture in such cases and the severe penalties for those who went beyond or broke these rules. But this fact has not prevented the popular myth of the ubiquitous and horror-movie Inquisition.

The Inquisition investigated accusations of heresy but also heard cases involving adultery and fornication, acute blasphemy, and – important this – clergy who were corrupt or immoral. The accused was not allowed to know the identity of the accuser but this was not, as we might think, so as to allow anonymous and irresponsible denunciations but to protect the accuser – there had been numerous examples of accusers being murdered and their families attacked. As a balance or form of judicial fairness, the accused were asked to provide a list of all their known enemies, and this group was then investigated to see if there was any ulterior motive involved in the accusation. If the accused was found guilty and refused to recant, he would be handed over to the secular arm for judgment and punishment. One who recanted and then fell again into heresy could not save himself by recanting again.[15]

In fact, almost all that we hear about the Inquisition is not about the general series of Church courts that existed and were Inquisitions but about one country and one body in particular: the Spanish Inquisition. Most of the images we have of the Inquisition have their origins in how we regard the Spain of the fifteenth and sixteenth centuries. In a recent pair of movies about the life of Queen Elizabeth 1 of England, the Spaniards lived not only in metaphorical but literal darkness – apparently the Spanish court, and of course the Vatican, never discovered the secret of window light or managed to purchase an adequate supply of candles. They also shouted all the time. So whereas good Queen Bess danced, laughed, and called for universal tolerance and mutual respect, the Catholics spent their days hurting people and plotting invasions.[16] They may be just movies but movies influence far more people than do serious ideas seriously discussed. That Queen Elizabeth tortured innocent Catholic priests and had them executed by hanging, drawing, and quartering seems to have escaped the producer of the risible films. But that's entirely understandable in that they were merely reflecting the popular image of history. Elizabeth used the most vile form of execution one can imagine – her victims were hanged but cut down while still alive, disembowelled and castrated while still conscious, and then watched as their innards were burned. They were then beheaded, their body cut into four parts and distributed in four corners of the city. Elizabeth's father, Henry VIII, was worse and murdered entire towns and villages that dared to question his anti-Roman Catholic reformation. Gentle and pious men who had never lifted a finger, let alone a weapon, in violence were starved, racked, beaten, and then murdered in public. Yet still we hold to the idea that nobody was as cruel as those Catholics in Spain and their papal and priestly masters.

The Spanish Inquisition was established in the fifteenth century and modelled on the papal courts that already existed in Europe precisely because Spain and the Spanish Church were profoundly threatened by a reality that was intrinsic to its foundation. The country had been taken back from the Muslims and from Muslim armies and subsequently united but found itself a Catholic state with a large Jewish and Islamic minority. There were, by the way, hardly any Protestants in Spain, and the myth of good, Christian reformers dying in flames in their thousands is utter nonsense. The Pope did give his total support to the Spanish Inquisition in its early days, but it soon became an organ of the Spanish state and the Spanish monarchy and was to a certain extent soiled by all the politics and personal ambitions that secular power and secular ambition in particular introduce to any struggle.

The reason for the foundation of the Inquisition was the challenge of the large number of conversos, people who had left Islam and in particular Judaism for Christianity – some of them were new or recent Catholics, others came from families where parents or grandparents had converted. Both Muslims and Jews were in a highly unfair position. To participate fully in the emerging Catholic Spain, and to make any meaningful advance in Spanish society, they were far better off as Christians; tolerance varied from region to region and era to era, but it was never advantageous to be non-Catholic in a country that increasingly linked religion with citizenship. The Spanish Catholic position was also challenging – the unified state was a recent development, still tenuous and threatened by a Muslim world determined to regain the Iberian Peninsula. Muslims in Spain obviously were suspected of divided loyalties, and Jews were often mistrusted since some Jews in Spain considered Islamic rule preferable to Christian.[17] It was a genuinely volatile situation made even less stable by ample doses of paranoia and insecurity.

Many Jews and Muslims, however, had made serious and heartfelt conversions to Catholicism and were devoted members of the Church. Queen Isabel's confessor was Fray Hernando de Talavera, the Archbishop of Granada and grandson of a Jewish woman. He was one of the royal family's most trusted and loved advisers. The bishop appointed by the monarchy to introduce sweeping reforms to the Spanish church was Alonso de Burgos, also from a converso family. Numerous highly successful converts rose to prominence in the Church and in civil, secular society. But there were also many who converted who either had no intention of being practising Catholics or who soon fell away from their faith. Most of these men and women simply became indifferent to Catholicism and organized religion in general while others continued to worship as Jews and – certainly a minority – actively mocked and abused their supposed new beliefs. All of this behaviour made life particularly difficult for genuine converts, who were treated with growing suspicion by the mainstream of Catholic Spain. To give some perspective on all this, in the southern city of Seville, then the largest in the country, at the beginning of the Inquisition at least half if not the majority of the population had until fairly recently been or were still non-Catholic. Catholic Spaniards and Spaniards of older Catholic ancestry were frightened and had some reason to be – massacres had occurred in living memory when minority populations aided Muslim armies. There was a heartfelt popular outcry for something to be done to protect both Catholic people and the Catholic faith.

Some of the figures for what occurred in Spain after the Inquisition was created are revealing. Isabel of Spain reigned for thirty years during what is regarded as the height of the Inquisition, and in that period some two thousand people were burned at the stake for heresy, while more than fifteen thousand were convicted of professing Catholicism but denying their faith and then took advantage of the Inquisition's offer and came back into the Church. Nobody would claim that judicial killing in the name of religion was justified but we need to appreciate that at this same time tens of thousands of people were maimed, whipped, beaten, and killed by the secular authorities for what we would now consider to be relatively minor crimes.

Public confessions of guilt and reconciliations with the Church were known as auto-de-fe, which means "act of faith" and did not signify burnings. That some of the changes of heart were the product of torture and pressure is beyond question, but it's also true that all sorts of people were persuaded by argument – religious figures of the magnitude of St. Ignatius of Loyola, St. John of the Cross, and St. Teresa of Avila may not have undergone the auto-de-fe but, like many others, were questioned by the Inquisition and then completely exonerated.[18]

There were certainly abuses, but one of the most infamous leaders of the Spanish Inquisition, Tomas de Torquemada, is a good example of someone who has been painted by history as a cynical and relentless sadist. Determined and dedicated he may have been, but Torquemada seldom used torture and went to great lengths to make sure that accuser and accused received justice. It would not have been difficult to kill at random and without trial, as happened elsewhere in Europe and would happen horribly often in the future. Remember, although Spain was a flawed society, it did not face the bloody civil wars of religion experienced in Germany, England, France, and the Low Countries and through most of the continent in the late sixteenth and mid-seventeenth centuries. The Spanish Inquisition had its last breaths in the 1720s, when it launched a campaign against Jewish converts but was dormant after this period and was closed by the monarchy in 1834. Rather like the Crusades, the history and memory of the Inquisition did not play a major part in affairs until the mid-nineteenth century, when anti-Catholic writers brought it back into the public square and used and distorted it to attack the Church. It's ironic that leading modern atheists criticize Christianity by reference to the Inquisition when it was non-Catholic Christians who originally resurrected the story of the Inquisition for their own internecine battles. Anachronism is no friend to good history. What we see or think of as self-evident and always to be aspired to – concepts such as freedom of worship, human rights, and so on – did not exist during the time of the Inquisition, and we should remember that many if not all of these advances came about due to the work of the Roman Catholic Church. But then whatever we may say in explanation or even partial defence of the Inquisition, runs the argument, it must never be forgotten that it did condemn Galileo and that the Roman Catholic Church is, naturally, the enemy of science and progress.

Actually, what we really need to remember about Galileo is that most of the people who use his name in argument could barely spell it, let alone tell us what actually happened to the man. His case is used over and over again because critics can't think of any other scientists who were mistreated by the Church. And in this instance they're right. There may have been some people in the scientific world who did not enjoy Church support and were even challenged by Catholicism but, sorry to disappoint, there weren't very many of them. The Church has been the hand-maiden of science and scientific discovery, and those who refer to Galileo tend to forget that Louis Pasteur, the inventor of pasteurization, was a devout Catholic, as was Alexander Fleming, who gave us penicillin. Or Father Nicolaus Copernicus, who first proposed the theory of the earth revolving around the sun – this was precisely what Galileo stated, but Copernicus taught it as theory and not fact. Or Monsignor Georges Henri Joseph Édouard Lemaître, a Belgian Roman Catholic priest and professor of physics at the Catholic University of Leuven, who proposed what became known as the Big Bang theory of the origin of the Universe. In the field of acceleration, Fr. Giambattista

Riccioli changed the way we understand that particular science; the father of modern Egyptology was Fr. Athanasius Kircher, and the Yugoslavian Fr. Roger Boscovich was the founder of modern atomic theory.

The man considered the father of genetics is the great Gregor Mendel. This University of Vienna–trained mathematician conducted a variety of complex experiments in the mid-nineteenth century, the most famous and important of which was the growing of pea plants over an eight-year period and his exploration of their genetic code, with great and lasting success in the area of genetics. He was a Catholic monk and later became abbot of his monastery. The Lutheran convert Fr. Nicholas Steno is one of the founders of geology and Fr. J.B. Macelwane's *Introduction to Theoretical Seismology* was the first American textbook on the subject. It was Roman Catholic clergy who took Western science to China, India, and Latin America.[19]

Catholic priests as well as Catholic laypeople have contributed to science with staggering success. Even before the nineteenth century, the Jesuits in particular, according to Jonathan Wright in his seminal book on the order, "had contributed to the development of pendulum clocks, pantographs, barometers, reflecting telescopes and microscopes, to scientific fields as various as magnetism, optics and electricity. They observed, in some cases before anyone else, the colored bands on Jupiter's surface, the Andromeda nebula and Saturn's rings. They theorized about the circulation of the blood (independently of Harvey), the theoretical possibility of flight, the way the moon effected the tides, and the wave-like nature of light. Star maps of the southern hemisphere, symbolic logic, flood-control measures on the Po and Adige rivers, introducing plus and minus signs into Italian mathematics – all were typical Jesuit achievements, and scientists as influential as Fermat, Huygens, Leibniz and Newton were not alone in counting Jesuits among their most prized correspondents."[20] So Catholicism and science and scientific breakthrough have not been in conflict but lived in mutual regard. It's particularly scandalous that many of the most vocal of those who condemn what they believe to be Catholic anti-scientific bigotry are frequently part of a political left that tends to ally itself with an animal rights movement that resists using animals for scientific progress and even threatens or actually attacks scientists who do so.

Which brings us back to Galileo. The Inquisition was rarely involved in the area of science, despite this well-known case. Galileo's trial was in 1663, and he was condemned not because of some scientific breakthrough and not because the Catholic Church – contrary to the modern version of events – was determined to resist change and progress because it feared a loss of power and control. Galileo was challenged because he declared a theory to be a fact and argued with the Church about the genuine meaning of the Bible. In 1992, Pope John Paul II apologized for the Church's treatment of Galileo and described the denunciation as a "tragic error." In 2008, Pope Benedict emphasized the importance of the scientist and praised his achievements. But acknowledgement of past wrongs and contrition are the last things wanted by critics of the Church. Far better to throw the Galileo chant around than listen to an organization explain that in this instance it did not behave according to its usually exemplary standards.

It would be easier if the case was straightforward, but, just like science, it requires a bit of effort to understand. During Galileo's life, the Catholic Church was at the centre of scientific discovery and sponsored scientists both in Rome and throughout the Catholic world, just as was the case before Galileo and would be afterwards. Indeed, Nicolaus Copernicus dedicated his seminal work, *On the Revolution of the Celestial Orbs,* to Pope Paul III. This honour is important because the book outlined Copernicus's theories concerning heliocentrism, the astronomical theory that the earth and other planets revolve around the stationary sun, which is at the centre of the universe. Geocentrism is a theory that claims the opposite. Heliocentrism wasn't a new idea, having first been proposed as early as the third century BC by Aristarchus of Samos. Copernicus was a Catholic and a priest, his brother an Augustinian monk who became a canon, and his sister a Benedictine nun who became a prioress. It wasn't the reaction of the Catholic Church that concerned Copernicus but the emerging Protestantism of the mid-sixteenth century. Because of his concerns about the Lutheran response and Martin Luther's known opposition to heliocentrism, he asked the Protestant pastor Andreas Osiander to ease his book into Protestant circles and explain its context to the leaders of the Reformation. Osiander went further than planned and wrote a preface that distorted Copernicus's views and described heliocentrism as a mere idea that more easily ex- plained the relationship between the sun and the earth. So we have a central book in the history of the new science dedicated to the Pope but diluted and altered when shown to Protestant leaders in case it caused offence. Something similar occurred to the Protestant scientist Johannes Kepler when he wrote an analysis of Copernicus. He was rejected and even condemned by other Protestant scholars and theologians but welcomed by the Catholic and particularly the Jesuit intelligentsia.

None of this is considered when the name and example of Galileo is used to dismiss the Church as reactionary and anti-scientific. The reality is that while heliocentrism was discussed and often accepted within Catholic circles – it was effectively the only place where it could be – the more traditional view of the solar system still prevailed even among leading scientists. So it's hardly a surprise that Galileo's Catholic judges had difficulty accepting his views, especially when they saw themselves as defending scientific orthodoxy and were supported in this by the scientific establishment. Aristotle had rejected heliocentricity and although, as we've seen, Copernicus and Kepler challenged him, they were far ahead of their time and were not always taken seriously by some of the leading scientists of the day. Today we can prove and disprove things with an ease that would have boggled the mind a hundred years ago, let alone in the seventeenth century. It's not only ignorant but supremely arrogant to believe that knowledge is constant. Even Galileo couldn't prove heliocentricity and in particular failed to counter the very argument that had been made by Aristotle two thousand years earlier. The Greek philosopher's position was that if heliocentrism was indeed true, we would be able to observe it by obvious shifts in the positions of the stars as the earth moved around the sun. Obviously the equipment required to prove this did not exist in the time of Aristotle or Galileo because of the enormous distance from the earth to the stars. Remember, the Church's claim is quite specific – not to be an infallible source of wisdom or to know scientific truths long before they have been discovered but to be the body and teaching office founded and left to us by Christ to communicate the Gospel, spread the word of Christianity, and save sinners. That it provided and provides a culture and context for other, secular truths to be propagated is a by-product and not the essence of its existence.

The science of Galileo's time was limited, and the entirely

reasonable view from intelligent observation was that the earth and the stars were not moving at all, but that the sun, moon, and stars were. Galileo was asked to prove his theory using the best scientific methods of the period but could not do so. Numerous colleagues thought he had failed. Scientific disagreement was encouraged in the Church, and far more radical ideas than those of Galileo had been offered for more than a century. He alienated fellow scientists by his insistence that his observations were true, that they were fact, that they were established, and that any alternative was not only totally wrong but the product of weak thinking and incompetent analysis. Galileo got into trouble because he maintained that since the new discoveries seemed to contradict scripture, those passages of scripture should be reinterpreted in a metaphorical way. He did not seek to oppose the Church nor to doubt the inspiration of scripture. The problem is that he abandoned science and started talking theology and so attracted the notice of the Roman Inquisition. If he had left theology out of his writings and discussions he would probably never have had problems. And he remained a faithful and devout Catholic to the end of his life. Other scientists urged him not to play the theologian, not necessarily out of fear but because they considered it to be hubris on his part – why, they asked, would you make this a matter of faith when the Church has supported and financed your and our work and provided a safe, encouraging environment for scientific research? Priests and bishop friends of Galileo made the same argument. The theory may well be true, they believed, and, if so, in time it would be accepted as such. The man was not to be turned. This new truth, he said, contradicted scripture.

By 1614, various priests had responded to his attacks. They said that the 93rd and 104th Psalms contradicted heliocentrism, as does Joshua – "And the sun stood still, and the moon stayed" – and others passages in the Bible. This wasn't good theology, certainly not good Catholicism. At the heart of Roman Catholicism is the belief that although the Bible is central to the faith, it requires interpretation and is part but not all of the beliefs of a Christian. Literal interpretation without context is not only dangerous but contrary to what the Bible teaches. We need to remember that this was only a few years before all the sectarian toxins flowing through the European bloodstream would throw the continent into a fever of self-destruction. War between Protestant and Catholic would ravage the land for thirty years. The Protestant Reformation had destabilized not only Europe but the Church itself. The Catholic response to the strict, Bible-alone notions of Protestantism produced saints, scholars, and reformers who graced Catholicism but also caused tumult and uncertainty. At a time when all seemed threatened, there were powerful men in the Church who found Galileo's taunts too much to tolerate.[21]

Pope Paul v met with Galileo, and, while not unsympathetic, refused to deal with the matter any further. The Galileo controversy was given to the Holy Office, which officially condemned Galileo's theory in 1616 and hoped that the entire debate would now disappear. It should be stressed that it was Galileo rather than the Church who refused to allow the wound to heal. Cardinal Robert Bellarmine, a Jesuit, a friend of science, and an internationally respected theologian and scholar, tried to reach a compromise when he issued a document that purposely said different things to different people. Galileo, it said, could not hold or argue the position but could explore and discuss it. It was an attempt to allow Galileo room to work without officially supporting his criticisms of the Church. This remained in place until 1623 when Galileo approached the new Pope and an old friend, Urban VIII. Maffeo Barberini had been and remained a patron of the arts and a supporter of scientific investigation. He had long encouraged Galileo both as a friend and as a cardinal and now, as Pope, tried to help him further. He strongly advised Galileo to approach the entire situation extremely carefully and to outline, as a good scholar should, the arguments both for and against the theory. It's never been fully explained why Galileo reacted so churlishly to this sound advice from a man who not only had befriended him but had defended him as well. Instead of pursuing his work, Galileo appeared to seek confrontation and attempted to humiliate the Pope. In his book *Dialogue on the Two World Systems,* he used the Pope's advice to present both sides of the debate but had Urban's position advocated by the fictional Simplicio, making fun of the character and the argument and making the Pope a figure of fun in the eyes of the academic world. It is said that Urban was truly hurt and felt betrayed by someone he had trusted and loved. Galileo also attacked the Jesuits and their astronomers, who had gone to great lengths to write and speak in his defence. Galileo was not some innocent, impotent victim standing up for truth and being persecuted by ignorant and violent people but an activist intent on conflict who repeatedly rejected offers of compromise.

Galileo eventually publicly recanted his views and ostensibly rejected heliocentrism but not, as is popularly assumed, because he was tortured. It is astounding how many people, including those who claim some knowledge of history, science, and the Church, make this claim as though it were absolute truth. Galileo was not tortured and was not even treated particularly badly. Ambassador Nicolini, the leading Tuscan diplomat in Rome, was a close friend of Galileo and wrote extensively about the case. If he had a bias, it was in favour of Galileo and against the Vatican. He sent regular reports to the court regarding affairs in Rome. Many of his letters dealt with the ongoing controversy surrounding Galileo, and he reported to his king that "the pope told me that he had shown Galileo a favour never accorded to another" and that "he has a servant and every convenience." The infamous image of a prisoner being shown the instruments of torture is sadly true – it was standard legal practice at the time – but they were not used on Galileo and not even seriously threatened. As we saw earlier with the authentic history of the Inquisition, entire books of laws, statutes, and case precedents dealt with what was allowed and not allowed in these cases, and *The Directory for Inquisitors* of 1595 prevented torture in such circumstances. If the laws surrounding torture had been broken, those responsible would have faced severe punishment.

The entire Galileo episode reveals both scientist and Church as less than perfect but says relatively little about the Church's attitude toward science. If we want long-term evidence of an ideology controlling and oppressing science, we'd be better off looking to the great atheist regimes of the twentieth century. Stalin actually had his scientists lie about their discoveries to the point where they in turn lied to him and as a result entire government policy was sometimes based on fraudulent research. The Soviets after Stalin and then under the supposedly more benign rule of Khrushchev and Brezhnev used psychiatry as a form of torture, incarcerating political dissidents under the guise that they were mentally ill, with the full backing of many in the scientific establishment.[22] The atheist, cultist Hitler was obsessed with the use of science to support his theories of eugenics, social engineering, and so-called racial health. One of the great ironies of the Galileo mess is that the famous play about his life that did so much to portray the Church as evil and terrified of change was written by Bertolt Brecht – a committed and doctrinaire Communist who publicly championed Soviet and East German Communism while free-thinking doctors, scientists, and researchers were being arrested and tortured and medicine was being used as a tool of the truly dictatorial state. But then hypocritical playwrights declaring war on the Church is far from unique, as we shall see.

If any issue requires and demands sensitivity and empathy, it is the Holocaust or the Shoah, the organized, systematic attempt at the genocide of the Jewish people, the extermination of gypsies and the handicapped, and the casual slaughter of what were considered lesser races and political and social opponents. The Holocaust stands as a ghastly icon of sophisticated and racist brutality. That it was initiated and performed by one of the most advanced nations and people in the world, with the help or indifference of so many other neighbours, races, governments, and states, makes it even more repugnant. Only a lunatic or a political sadist would question the reality of what happened, but, tragically, there is a renaissance in Holocaust denial, particularly in some parts of the Islamic world. To deny is bestial but to explain is quintessentially human. And absolutely essential.

The accusations are legion. The Church is anti-Semitic, the Pope did nothing to oppose Hitler or save the Jews and sometimes even collaborated, and local Catholic leaders aided the Hitler regime. Why, the attack continues, did the Pope not excommunicate Nazis and speak out publicly against the Jewish persecution? The Church, we are then told, contributed and often created the Jew-hating culture of Europe that led to the Holocaust and even now refuses to admit its errors in this regard. This is horribly wrong, simplistic, and irresponsible if not callous. All sorts of powerful people and bodies did far too little to help the Jews during the Second World War – the Western democracies were ambivalent on the issue, socialist and communist parties frequently collaborated with Nazi racism, and an entire Protestant church was created in Germany to inject a perverse theological credibility into National Socialism. The Roman Catholic Church, on the other hand and as we will see, did almost all that it could and suffered terribly as a result. Remember that beyond the six million Jews who were murdered by the Nazis were the six million non-Jews also murdered, many of them Catholics and hundreds of thousands of them Catholic priests, activists, and resisters.[23]

This view that the Church was on the right side, the good side, the moral side, the anti-Nazi side, was standard in the years following 1945, and it was only in the mid-1960s and as part of a concerted campaign to libel Catholicism that attitudes toward Catholic opposition to Hitlerism changed. The positive image of the Church during the war was so enthusiastic and overwhelming that the World Jewish Congress donated a great deal of money to the Vatican in gratitude for what it had done, and in 1945 Rabbi Herzog of Jerusalem thanked Pope Pius "for his lifesaving efforts on behalf of the Jews during the occupation of Italy." He continued, "The people of Israel will never forget what His Holiness and his illustrious delegates, inspired by the eternal principles of religion, which form the very foundation of true civilization, are doing for our unfortunate brothers and sisters in the most tragic hour of our history, which is living proof of Divine Providence in this world." When the Pope died in 1958, Golda Meir, then Israeli foreign minister, later prime minister and a national hero and symbol in her country, delivered a eulogy at the United Nations praising the man for his work on behalf of her people. "We share in the grief of humanity [at the death of Pius XII]," she said. "When fearful martyrdom came to our people in the decade of Nazi terror, the voice of the pope was raised for the victims. The life of our times was enriched by a voice speaking out on the great moral truths above the tumult of daily conflict. We mourn a great servant of peace." Rabbi Louis Finkelstein, chancellor of the Jewish Theological Seminary of America, wrote, "No keener rebuke has come to Nazism than from Pope Pius XI and his successor, Pope Pius XII," and Rabbi Alexander Safran, the chief rabbi of Romania, stated: "In the most difficult hours of which we Jews of Romania have passed through, the generous assistance of the Holy See . . . was decisive and salutary. It is not easy for us to find the right words to express the warmth and consolation we experienced because of the concern of the supreme pontiff, who offered a large sum to relieve the sufferings of deported Jews. . . . The Jews of Romania will never forget these facts of historic importance."[24]

After hearing the Pope's Christmas address of 1941, the *Times* wrote: "The voice of Pius XII is a lonely voice in the silence and darkness enveloping Europe this Christmas. . . . In calling for a 'real new order' based on 'liberty, justice and love' . . . the pope put himself squarely against Hitlerism." Moshe Sharett, who became Israel's first foreign minister and later second prime minister, said, "I told [Pope Pius XII] that my first duty was to thank him, and through him the Catholic Church, on behalf of the Jewish public for all they had done in the various countries to rescue Jews. . . . We are deeply grateful to the

Catholic Church." Albert Einstein, one of the most famous Jewish figures in world history and a man who was offered the presidency of Israel, said, "Only the Catholic Church protested against the Hitlerian onslaught on liberty. Up till then I had not been interested in the Church, but today I feel a great admiration for the Church, which alone has had the courage to struggle for spiritual truth and moral liberty." Another Jewish man was closer to the relevant events than almost anyone. In 1945, the chief rabbi of Rome, Israel Zolli, publicly embraced Roman Catholicism, taking the baptismal name of Eugenio in honour of the Pope. This extraordinary and controversial conversion was partly due to Zolli's admiration for the Pope's sheltering and saving of Italian Jews.[25]

For twenty years it was considered a self-evident truth that the Church was a member of the victim class during the Second World War, and Pope Pius was mentioned with Churchill and Roosevelt as part of a triumvirate of anti-fascism. So how did all this change? In 1963, German writer Rolf Hochhuth's play *The Deputy* was first performed. Hochhuth was a committed anti-Catholic – he later championed the notorious British Holocaust-denier, revisionist historian, and convicted criminal David Irving – and his long, unwieldy, and actually seldom-seen play accused Pope Pius XII of being too frightened and cowardly to speak out against the Nazis and their anti-Semitism. The play was acid in its condemnation of the papacy, but the author himself admitted privately and in interviews that Pius in reality did a great deal for the Jewish people. But fiction battled fact at a time when the Catholic Church was analyzing itself to an alarming degree and a liberal, secular wave was beginning to gain motion in Europe and North America. These were the beginnings of the permissive age, and the Catholic Church was emerging as a major obstacle to social and sexual change as well as to cultural relativism. A mingling of Soviet opposition to Catholicism, a new secularism, and Western liberal doubts about absolutes and religious prohibitions all contributed to the attack on the Church's role in the Holocaust. One fairly obscure play could not have changed very much on its own but it did perhaps symbolize a new mood that was to distort truth and create a historical fairy tale.

The Catholic Church's opposition to Adolf Hitler and Nazism began long before 1939 or the beginnings of the Holocaust. On April 28, 1935, Eugenio Maria Giuseppe Giovanni Pacelli, later Pope Pius XII, spoke to more than a quarter of a million people in Lourdes, the place of the nineteenth-century appearances of the Virgin Mary to the young Bernadette. These were pilgrims from all over the world, who were likely to take any message they heard from a papal representative back to their home countries. Pacelli told them that the German Nazis "are in reality only miserable plagiarists who dress up old errors with new tinsel. It does not make any difference whether they flock to the banners of social revolution, whether they are guided by a false concept of the world and of life, or whether they are possessed by the superstition of a race and blood cult." What is notable about this speech is that it wasn't notable. Pacelli had made other such speeches in public and in private meetings had repeatedly expressed his opposition to Nazism and concerns about the rise of racism. The Berlin regime was well aware of this and considered Pacelli even as problematic as the pope, Pius XI, who in 1937 wrote an entire papal encyclical, *Mit Brennender Sorge*, outlining the dangers and horrors of Nazi ideology. The following year, Pacelli told a group of Belgian pilgrims that "it is impossible for a Christian to take part in anti-Semitism.

Anti-Semitism is inadmissible; spiritually, we are all Semites."[26]

The accepted view within elite political circles was that Rome was if anything too aggressively anti-Hitler, and some German Catholics were concerned that their position could be made difficult if not impossible if the Vatican maintained its position. It has been said that the Vatican had already set a theme by its support for the anti-government forces in Spain. While it's true that when thousands of Roman Catholic priests, nuns, and bishops were being murdered by the Republicans in Spain, the Church did, understandably, show some support for the Nationalists, but this was in defence and protection of Catholicism and Catholics and had nothing to do with fascism. The Vatican did not, in fact, give official backing to Franco or the Nationalists as such but did call for an end to the slaughter of its adherents, which is what it was supposed to do and what any other organization would have done as well. Nazism, anyway, was something entirely different from the archaic monarchism of the Spanish right. This may not seem obvious to anti-Catholic writers seventy years after the fact, but it was clearly evident at the time. Dr. Joseph Lichten was a Polish Jewish diplomat who later worked for the Anti-Defamation League of B'nai B'rith. He wrote, "Pacelli had obviously established his position clearly, for the Fascist governments of both Italy and Germany spoke out vigorously against the possibility of his election to succeed Pius XI in March of 1939, though the cardinal secretary of state had served as papal nuncio in Germany from 1917 to 1929." And "the day after his election, the Berlin *Morgenpost* said: 'The election of cardinal Pacelli is not accepted with favor in Germany because he was always opposed to Nazism and practically determined the policies of the Vatican under his predecessor.'"

The German government campaigned against the election of Pacelli to the papacy, both through its diplomats and friends in the Vatican and Italy and also by threats and pressure. He was considered to be the main adviser to the Pope on Nazism and to have shaped much of the anti-Nazi policies of the Vatican. Pacelli himself made more than forty speeches in Germany condemning Nazism; spoke, wrote, and broadcast against Hitler's ideas long before the Austrian came to power in 1933; and refused to ever meet the Nazi leader. Touching on this refusal of Pius XII to shake the Fuehrer's hand, one of the most notorious attacks on him in recent years was made by British author John Cornwell in his book *Hitler's Pope*. The original dust jacket of the highly criticized and often discredited book shows Pacelli leaving a building and walking past what appear to be Nazi storm troopers. This, of course, is why the picture was used. But it is actually a 1927 picture of Pacelli long before he was elected Pope, the soldiers are of the Weimar Republic army, and the ceremony Pacelli is leaving is in honour of President Hindenburg. Supporters of the book and critics of the Pope responded at the time and later that this was explained inside the book. Quite so. For the vast majority of people looking at the thing, they see what appears to be a Pope marching past Nazi guards and do not read some obscure explanation. That, surely, was the purpose. It offers an encapsulation in a single picture of the entire campaign against a good and brave man.

The Reich's Chief Security Service gave its informed opinion of the newly elected Pope in 1939: "Pacelli has already made himself prominent by his attacks on National Socialism during his tenure as Cardinal Secretary of State, a fact which earned him the hearty approval of the Democratic States during the papal elections." His first encyclical was *Summi Pontificatus,* which condemned Nazism and stated, quoting St. Paul, that in the Catholic Church there is "neither Gentile nor Jew, circumcision nor uncircumcision."

Hitler's attitude toward the Roman Catholic Church wavered between contempt and anger; at times he told colleagues that the Church would wither away to nothing more than a collection of powerless old women but then he would rage against what he saw as the most organized and dangerous opposition to his plans. He may have been baptized as a Catholic but this was irrelevant to him, and the notion that Nazism was in some way an offshoot or product of Christianity is quite the leap. Although some anti-Semites at the time may have been influenced by a perversion of Christian teaching or the misplaced ideas of Christians, National Socialism itself was pagan and cultist. Leading Nazi ideologues blamed Jews more for their giving the world Christ and Christianity than for their Judaism or perceived characteristics – something akin to why Voltaire was so anti-Semitic a century and a half earlier. Christianity was weak and forgiving, the Nazi interpretation of north European paganism was strong and relentless, Jesus was a Jew and preached love, the northern gods were Aryan and demanded war.

Shortly after the outbreak of the Second World War, Joachim Von Ribbentrop, Berlin's most persuasive and ostensibly civilized diplomat, made a visit to see Pope Pius. The Nazi ambassador explained that Germany would certainly win the war, that the Pope was being foolish to support the Western democracies, and that any defeat of Nazism was a victory for Communism – this argument that godless, atheistic Bolshevism was the only alternative to Nazism would be used repeatedly to try to persuade the Church to change sides. The Pope listened quietly while Von Ribbentrop spoke and then produced a large folder that listed numerous persecutions, atrocities, and illegalities carried out by the Nazis. He read them out calmly and in perfect German and then waited for a response. None was forthcoming.[27]

One of the accusations made against the Pope is that he did not give a public and obvious denunciation of anti-Semitism during the Holocaust. It's a valid issue but one that is often discussed with too little understanding of the reality of 1940s Europe. Such explicit condemnations of Nazi anti-Semitism were not really made in London, Washington, or Moscow, but it's always assumed that Rome should somehow have been different, in spite of the fact that the Vatican was surrounded by Nazi or pro-Nazi troops and that millions of Roman Catholics lived under Nazi occupation whereas London, Washington, and even Moscow were relatively cocooned and the latter even comparatively safe. Actually the Pope did make numerous condemnations of Nazi racism, both before and during the war. A public statement, however, was not without consequences and was not at all guaranteed to achieve the desired outcome. One clear case of the tragedy of this act and something that influenced the papal position was what occurred in Holland when the Archbishop of Utrecht preached against the Nazi treatment of Dutch Jews. He had been ordered not to do so but decided that he had no option. In direct response, the Nazis rounded up not only Jews but Jewish converts to Catholicism, including the Carmelite nun and noted philosopher Edith Stein, who died at Auschwitz concentration camp and later was named as a Catholic saint. In his vitally important book *Three Popes and the Jews,* the Jewish theologian, historian, and Israeli diplomat Pinchas E. Lapide recounts the case of a German Jewish family who managed to escape their homeland for neutral Spain. Like many others, they were able to escape death due to the intervention of the Pope and his staff. They wrote, "None of us wanted the Pope to take an open stand. We were all fugitives, and fugitives do not wish to be pointed at. The Gestapo would have become more excited and would have intensified its inquisitions. If the Pope had protested, Rome would have become the center of attention. It was better that the Pope said nothing. We all shared this opinion at the time, and this is still our conviction today."

When the Germans directly occupied Rome, the papacy and Nazi troops were, quite literally, within each other's sight. We now know that Hitler had compiled plans to kidnap Pius.[28] In 1943, the Pope may not have been aware of this danger, but he certainly knew that the Germans were prepared to use force to enter the Vatican and had murdered Catholic clerics and leaders all over Europe. The context says so much when we consider the Pope's reaction to the Nazi policy toward the Jews of Rome. First, in September 1943, the Germans demanded one hundred pounds of gold within three days or three hundred Jews would be arrested. The Jewish community could raise only two-thirds of the gold so turned to the Church. Pope Pius smuggled the city's chief rabbi into the city and had him taken straight to the Vatican treasury, where he was given what he needed. Tragically, and typically, the payment only postponed the inevitable.

When it became obvious that the Nazis intended to round up and deport Rome's Jews, the Pope became arguably the most active protector of the Jewish people of any regional dignitary in occupied Europe throughout the Second World War. Between 4,000 and 7,000 Jews were hidden in almost 200 refuges in Vatican City. Monasteries, churches, private homes, hospitals, and offices were used, and the Pope gave a personal order that everything must be done to make sure as many Jewish people as possible were sheltered from the Nazis. Castel Gandolfo, the Pope's summer residence, was put into use in the cause. Pinchas Lapide again: "In Rome we saw a list of 155 convents and monasteries – Italian, French, Spanish, English, American, and also German – mostly extraterritorial property of the Vatican . . . which sheltered throughout the German occupation some 5,000 Jews in Rome. No less than 3,000 Jews found refuge at one time at the Pope's summer residence at Castel Gandolfo; sixty lived for nine months at the Jesuit Gregorian University, and half a dozen slept in the cellar of the Pontifical Bible Institute." He also concluded after exhaustive research that Pius XII's Roman Catholic Church was more successful and active in rescuing and saving Jews than any other organization in Europe.[29]

Yet still the accusations of collaboration or at least the claims that the Pope did too little continued. Sir Martin Gilbert is one of the most respected historians in the world and a central voice in studies of the Holocaust and Israel. He wrote, "As a historian of the Holocaust I frequently receive requests from Jewish educators, seeking support for grant applications for their Holocaust programs. Almost all these applications include a sentence about how the new program will inform students that the Pope, and the Vatican, 'did nothing' during the Holocaust to help Jews. The most recent such portrayal reached me while I was writing this review. It is part of a proposal to a major Jewish philanthropic organization, and contains the sentence: 'Also discusses the role of the Vatican and the rabidly anti-Semitic Pope Pius XII, who were privy to information regarding the heinous crimes being committed against the Jews, and their indifferent response.' That the Pope and the Vatican were either silent by-standers, or even active collaborators in Hitler's diabolical plan – and 'rabidly anti-Semitic,' as stated above – has become something of a truism in Jewish educational circles, and a powerful, emotional assertion made by American-Jewish writers, lecturers, and educators." Gilbert acknowledges the Church's failing but stresses that, for example, "in France, leaders of the Roman Catholic clergy were outspoken in their condemnation of the deportations. In Italy, churchmen across the whole spectrum of Roman Catholicism, including leading Jesuits, saved Jews from deportation. Many hundreds of Polish priests and nuns are among more than 5,000 Catholic Poles who have been recognized by the state of Israel for their courage in saving Jews."

He continued, "Among Roman Catholic clergymen who helped save Jews was Archbishop Giovanni Montini, the future Pope Paul vi. When the government of Israel asked him, in 1955, to accept an award for his rescue work during the Holocaust, Montini replied: 'All I did was my duty. And besides I only acted upon orders from the Holy Father.' When the deportation of 80,000 Jews from Slovakia to Auschwitz began in March 1942, Pius authorized formal written protests by both the Vatican secretary of state and the papal representative in the Slovak capital, Bratislava. When a second round of deportations began in Slovakia the following spring, Pius wrote a letter of protest to the Slovak government. Dated April 7, 1943, it was outspoken and unambiguous. 'The Holy See has always entertained the firm hope,' Pius wrote, that the Slovak government 'would never proceed with the forcible removal of persons belonging to the Jewish race. It is, therefore, with great pain that the Holy See has learned of the continued transfers of such a nature from the territory of the republic.'"

Perhaps the most illuminating book about the Pope Pius controversy, and there have now been many, was written by Rabbi David G. Dalin in 2005. In *The Myth of Hitler's Pope* he writes poignantly that "very few of the many recent books about Pius XII and the Holocaust are actually about Pius XII and the Holocaust. The liberal bestselling attacks on the pope and the Catholic Church are really an intra-Catholic argument about the direction of the Church today. The Holocaust is simply the biggest club available for liberal Catholics to use against traditional Catholics in their attempt to bash the papacy and thereby to smash traditional Catholic teaching."[30] This is very much to the point and can be extended not just to anti-papal Catholics offended by the new orthodoxy of the Church but to anti-Catholics in greater society. What better way to marginalize a belief and an institution than by alleging that in one of the great battles of good against evil that institution was on the wrong side?

In a 2001 interview with the Vatican newspaper *L'Osservatore Romano,* Dalin stated, "Pope Pacelli was righteous among the nations, who must be recognized for having protected and saved hundreds of thousands of Jews. It is difficult to imagine that so many world Jewish leaders, in such different continents, could have been mistaken or confused when it came to praising the Pope's conduct during the War. Their gratitude to Pius XII lasted a long time, and it was genuine and profound." As this book was being completed, Dr. Michael Hesemann, a German historian carrying out research in the Vatican archives for the American inter-faith group Pave the Way Foundation, issued some of his findings and announced that "Pope Pius may have arranged the exodus of about 200,000 Jews from Germany just three weeks after Kristallnacht, when thousands of Jews were rounded up and sent to concentration camps." Commenting on the research, the chairman of the foundation, Elliot Hershberg, said: "Cardinal Eugenio Pacelli – the future Pius XII – wrote to Roman Catholic archbishops around the world to urge them to apply for visas for 'non-Aryan Catholics' and Jewish converts to Christianity who wanted to leave Germany. We believe that many Jews who were successful in leaving Europe may not have had any idea that their visas and travel documents were obtained through these Vatican efforts. . . . Everything we have found thus far seems to indicate the known negative perception of Pope Pius XII is wrong."[31]

We're certainly grateful to you, sir, but surely the larger question is why this "negative perception" of Pope Pius existed in the first place and why it was not only allowed to exist but often encouraged and fed in some circles. Commenting on the statements in the U.K.'s *Daily Telegraph,* Dr. Ed Kessler, director of the Cambridge-based Woolf Institute of Abrahamic Faiths, said, "It is clear that Pius XII facilitated the saving of Roman Jews."[32] Yes it is, and the Jews of so many others parts of the world as well. He was a righteous Gentile, he was a righteous Pope, he was a righteous Roman Catholic, he was a righteous man.

CATHOLICS
AND THEOLOGY

THE GREAT CATHOLIC communicator and popular theologian Archbishop Fulton J. Sheen once said that "there are not over a hundred people in the United States who hate the Catholic Church. There are millions, however, who hate what they wrongly believe to be the Catholic Church, which is, of course, quite a different thing." The same applies to people all over the world. If Roman Catholics genuinely believed all that they are condemned for believing, they would indeed deserve to be dismissed. Problem is, even many Catholics have very little idea of authentic Catholic belief, let alone committed or casual opponents of the faith. Because Catholic belief covers so many areas, this chapter will have to be exceedingly selective. Then again, critics are even more so. Catholicism is Christianity. Protestants, or at least genuine Protestants, argue that they found the ship of the Church covered with barnacles and weeds and gave it a good scrubbing and cleaning between the fifteenth and seventeenth centuries, revealing the original and authentic Christian faith. Wycliffe, Tyndale, Huss, Luther, Calvin, Zwingli, and the rest of the reformers got out their metaphorical soap and water and restored the Church to its Biblical, first-century form and shape. No papacy, no Vatican, no saints and feast days, no obsession with the Virgin Mary, but a reliance on the Bible alone and a conviction that men and women are saved by faith alone. There is no room here for an account of the Protestant Reformation, the rise of nationalism, the advent of the printing press, the emergence of capitalism, or a discussion of what Martin Luther in particular really wanted when he first began to question the Church. What we can say with confidence is that there are some inherent problems in the Protestant approach. If the Bible is the final word of God and the only guide to salvation and life, why are there tens of thousands of competing Protestant denominations and why are so many of them mutually exclusive? They all believe in the Bible and read it as believing and good followers of Christ. Yet some argue for the baptism of babies, others for the baptism of adults; some ordain women, others don't; some allow the consumption of alcohol, others don't; some believe that the Eucharist is the body of Christ, others that it is partly His body, others that it is deeply symbolic, others still that it is merely a gesture. Some Protestant churches believe that only a specific early seventeenth-century translation of the Bible is acceptable, others think they're wrong. Some allow divorce and even homosexuality, others not. And so on. Yet all claim the Bible as their inerrant guide.

The ecclesial sense of life in Christ is the fundamental point of departure between Catholicism and Protestantism, particularly in its evangelical form, and between Catholicism and Protestantism's bastard offspring, which is postmodern secularism. To put it bluntly, knowledge of Jesus is available to all people but to know Christ is available only to Christians in communion with the Church. To live in Christ is to live in a Church, to live in *the* Church, because that is how Christ in His spirit gives Himself to us. Jesus might be one's personal Lord and Saviour, but the result tends to be a Jesus who looks suspiciously like oneself. This leads the Roman Catholic Church to have a very different approach to scripture. Catholics, of course, know and acknowledge that the Bible is the word of God. They also know and acknowledge, however, that Jesus Christ did not leave us a Bible but left us a Pope and a teaching office, the Magisterium. Through the Pope and the teaching authority of the Church, the truth of the Bible is guided and guarded through the ages. Interpretation is not left to individuals but to those given the authority and the ability to interpret by Jesus Christ while He was on earth present here among us. In the New Testament, the names Simon, Peter, or Cephas are mentioned almost 200 times, while the names of all the other apostles combined are mentioned fewer than 140. Peter is mentioned first in the list of apostles by Matthew "to single him out as the most prominent one of the twelve." Throughout the New Testament, he is considered the leader of Christ's followers, and St. Paul later spent fifteen days with him as a preparation for his own journeys of conversion. But the most important event for Peter, and for us, was when Christ took him and the other apostles on a journey to, well, change his name.[1]

The place chosen was several days from the central ministry of Christ and His followers, far off in the northern tip of the country. Known in modern Israel as Banias and in the Bible as Caesarea Philippi, this area was remote, out of the way, and also supremely pertinent and important. It's a beautiful spot with a natural forest, a waterfall, and luscious rock formations. It was also considered one of the religious wonders of the ancient world and a pilgrimage site for ancient pagans. It had been used for animal and perhaps human sacrifice, and King Herod had built a temple to Caesar Augustus on top of the huge rock that still dominates the area. At the base of the rock was a deep, dark hole considered to be bottomless and known as the "gates of hell." It was before the pagan temple, before the gates of hell, before the place of sacrifice and ignorance that Christ, speaking in Aramaic, gives Simon, or Peter, the name Kepha, or Rock, being Petra in Greek or Peter in English. The exchange is deeply moving. Jesus asks His friends who people say He is. They reply that all sorts of ideas are circulating. That He is John the Baptist, that He is Elijah, Jeremiah, or one of the other prophets. This is all very flattering but entirely wrong. Jesus is the Messiah, but none of them say this because, while they love and revere Him, they do not recognize the Messiah promised by God in the Old Testament in this man they can see and hear. Christ accepts their reply and then turns to Simon Peter: "But what about you. Who do you say I am?"

Simon Peter does not hesitate. He has heard all the arguments, listened to the legalistic objections to Jesus and the explanations even from followers as to why He cannot be the chosen one. "You are the Anointed One. You are the Messiah. You are the Son of the Living God!" Then, from Jesus, "You are greatly blessed, Simon, Jonah's son, for this was not revealed to you through human means. This was revealed to you personally by my Father in heaven. You have heard all the human reasons why I am not good enough to be the Messiah, and you have rejected them all. Thus my Father has found your soul open to receiving the truth from him, and it is this you have just proclaimed." Jesus continues, "And so I now tell you that you are the Rock. On this rock I will build my Church, and the gates of Hell will not overcome it!" And then, "I will give you the keys of the kingdom of Heaven; whatever you bind on earth will be bound in heaven and whatever you loose on earth will be loosed in heaven."

The reference to the keys is taken from Isaiah and refers to the keys of the steward of the kingdom. The throne of King

David, however, had been vacant for almost six hundred years until the angel Gabriel had told Mary – as is recorded in the book of Luke – that her son would be given that Davidic throne, which once belonged to his "father David." Jesus is the new and final King of Israel and He appoints as His steward, as the man with total and complete authority of His Kingdom, His Church, and His followers, Peter who is the Rock. The steward was the King's representative while he was away and until he returned. The office was also successive and unchallenged in Israel among the Jewish people and passed down either by father to son or by appointment. In other words, although the individual holding the office of steward would die, the office itself would continue and would never diminish in authority or meaning. This might seem obscure to us, but Christ was speaking to Jews of the first century in a language and with symbols and metaphors that they would understand and appreciate. History was a living, breathing creature to a people who lived by the scriptures and knew their history as a guide to their future. They would have known exactly what Jesus was saying and why He was saying it. That, of course, is why He spoke what he did and where He did.[2]

Jesus also uses the image of a shepherd and his sheep. "When they had finished breakfast, Jesus said to Simon Peter, 'Simon, son of John, do you love me more than these?' He said to him, 'Yes, Lord, you know that I love you.' He said to him, 'Feed my lambs.' He then said to him a second time, 'Simon, son of John, do you love me?' He said to him, 'Yes, Lord, you know that I love you.' He said to him, 'Tend my sheep.' He said to him the third time, 'Simon, son of John, do you love me?' Peter was distressed that he had said to him a third time, 'Do you love me?' and he said to him, 'Lord, you know everything; you know that I love you.' [Jesus] said to him, 'Feed my sheep.'" Again, these were not words without meaning and not accidental or incidental references. Christ had a specific purpose in mind: to instruct His followers, who knew that "feed" and "tend" indicated teaching and ruling. Jesus is asking Peter, telling him, to shepherd His flock on earth, to govern the Church that He will leave. Thus it was Peter who would speak on behalf of the apostles, who would stand up at the birth of the Church at Pentecost to lead it, and who would be given the authority to forgive sins before the rest of the apostles. And in one of the most human and compelling passages of the Bible, he was the man who was slower than John when running to the empty tomb but who was allowed to enter first by John, who evidently acknowledged Peter's authority.

That the early Church accepted and acknowledged that Peter was the first Pope and that his successors possessed the teaching authority of the Church is documented from the earliest writings. In AD 170 Tatian the Syrian wrote, "Simon Kephas answered and said, 'You are the Messiah, the Son of the living God.' Jesus answered and said unto him, 'Blessed are you, Simon son of Jonah: flesh and blood has not revealed it unto thee, but my Father which is in heaven. And I say unto thee also, that you are Kephas, and on this Rock will I build my Church; and the gates of hades shall not prevail against it.'" Tetullian forty years later: "Was anything hid from Peter, who was called the Rock, whereon the Church was built; who obtained the keys of the Kingdom of Heaven, and the power of loosing and of binding in heaven and on earth?" St. Clement of Rome, the first apostolic father of the Church: "Be it known to you, my lord, that Simon [Peter], who, for the sake of the true faith, and the most sure foundation of his doctrine, was set apart to be the foundation of the Church, and for this end was by Jesus Himself, with His truthful mouth, named Peter." St. Hippolytus in AD 225: "Peter, the Rock of the Church . . . the Rock of the Faith, whom Christ our Lord called blessed, the teacher of the Church, the first disciple, he who has the Keys of the Kingdom."[3]

These quotations may seem esoteric but they represent the deepest feelings of the early Church, the early Christians, the people who risked and often faced martyrdom for their faith. This was not a version of Christianity but Christianity itself. Origen in the early and mid-third century: "See what the Lord said to Peter, that great foundation of the Church, and most solid Rock, upon which Christ founded the Church." And: "Look at [Peter], the great foundation of the Church, that most solid of rocks, upon whom Christ built the Church. And what does our Lord say to him? 'Oh you of little faith,' he says, 'why do you doubt?'" and "Upon him [Peter], as on the earth, the Church was founded." St. Cyprian in AD 246: "For first to Peter, upon whom He built the Church, and from whom He appointed and showed that unity should spring . . ." and "God is one, and Christ is one, and the Church is one, and the Chair [of Peter] is one, by the Lord's word, upon a Rock. . . ." St. Cyril of Jerusalem in AD 363: "Our Lord Jesus Christ then become man, but by the many He was not known. But wishing to teach that which was not known, having assembled His disciples, He asked, 'Who do you say that I the Son of man am?' . . . And all being silent, for it was beyond man to know, Peter, the Foremost of the Apostles, the Chief Herald of the Church, not using language of his own finding, but having his mind enlightened by the Father, says unto Him, 'Thou art the Christ,' and not simply that, but, 'the Son of the living God.' And a blessing follows the speech . . . and upon this Rock I will found my Church. . . .'"

St. Gregory in AD 370, St. Basil in AD 371, St. Epiphanius in AD 385, St. Ambrose of Milan in the same year, St. Asterius and St. John Chrysostom in AD 387, and St. Jerome in AD 393 all wrote that it was Peter who had been given the keys of the kingdom and the leadership of the Church and that this authority and position were passed to his successors. The great St. Augustine in AD 410: "These miserable wretches, refusing to acknowledge the Rock as Peter and to believe that the Church has received the Keys to the Kingdom of Heaven, have lost these very keys from their own hands" and, "Why! a faggot that is cut from the vine retains its shape. But what use is that shape if it is not living from the root? Come, brother, if you wish to be engrafted in the vine. It is grievous when we see you thus lying cut off. Number the bishops from the See of Peter. And, in that order of fathers, see whom succeeded whom. This is the Rock which the proud gates of hades do not conquer. All who rejoice in peace, only judge truly." The Council of Chalcedon in AD 451 ruled that "wherefore the most holy and blessed Leo, archbishop of the great and elder Rome, through us, and through this present most holy synod, together with the thrice blessed and all-glorious Peter the Apostle, who is the rock and foundation of the Catholic Church, and the foundation of the orthodox faith, has stripped him [Dioscorus] of the episcopate."[4]

Peter's place is sometimes denied by critics of papal supremacy and Catholic theology, who use the example of Paul seeming to challenge him: "But when Cephas came to Antioch, I opposed him to his face, because he stood self-condemned; for until certain people came from James, he used to eat with the Gentiles. But after they came, he drew back and kept himself separate for fear of the circumcision faction. And the other Jews joined him in this hypocrisy, so that even Barnabas was led astray by their hypocrisy. But when I saw that they were not acting consistently with the truth of the gospel, I said to Cephas before them all, 'If you, though a Jew, live like a Gentile and not like a Jew, how can you compel the Gentiles to live like Jews?'" Problem is, this is not a challenge to Peter's authority or his teaching but a criticism of his lifestyle. The man may sometimes fail but the teaching is something entirely different. And so to papal infallibility, which does not mean that if the Pope says it is raining it is raining or that if he promises some sporting victory for a favourite team it will happen. On a more serious note, it does not mean that papal comments and opinions, books and articles, views and sermons are without blemish, even though they are certainly worth regarding because of their source. Papal infallibility is quite specific.

Infallibility does not mean impeccability. Infallibility is a teaching about who the Lord is. He is Christ, who promised, "I will be with you to the end of the ages," and who will never let His Church fall into fundamental error. This is a teaching about the Holy Spirit in the Catholic Church. The Pope is not perfect and is not supposed or expected to be. There have been weak Popes and bad Popes – not many actually and nowhere near as many as is supposed to be the case but it would be foolish to argue that they have all been brave, pure, and brilliant. Nor is infallibility restricted to the Pope. It also applies to the body of bishops when they teach true doctrine. Critics of the Church often speak of Vatican II or the Second Vatican Council as the great "It's okay now and everything is forgiven," as though all that went before the 1960s was reactionary and wrong and all taught by the council and all that occurred afterwards light and progressive. Actually, the council didn't change very much at all, has often been misinterpreted and exploited and, anyway, was a legitimate gathering of the Church and as such simply another stage in Catholic history. It explained infallibility thus: "Although the individual bishops do not enjoy the prerogative of infallibility, they can nevertheless proclaim Christ's doctrine infallibly. This is so, even when they are dispersed around the world, provided that while maintaining the bond of unity among themselves and with Peter's successor, and while teaching authentically on a matter of faith or morals, they concur in a single viewpoint as the one which must be held conclusively. This authority is even more clearly verified when, gathered together in an ecumenical council, they are teachers and judges of faith and morals for the universal Church. Their definitions must then be adhered to with the submission of faith."[5]

As head of the bishops, the Pope obviously has a particular responsibility to and relationship with the Catholic world. When he makes a statement, there are certain absolute requirements essential for that pronouncement to be considered infallible. It has to be in the realm of faith and morals, and it has to be made while the Pope is speaking *ex cathedra,* or from the seat of Peter, the first Pope. This is not a literal but a metaphorical throne, and it's important to remember that the Pope speaking *ex cathedra* is extraordinarily rare. As we've seen above, Christ gave Peter and his spiritual successors the keys of the Church and promised him that when he taught and led as the steward of Christ on earth he would not, could not, commit error. We can dismiss Jesus if we like, but, logically, if we follow Him we ought to take what He said pretty seriously. Those who lived in Peter's time did. They certainly understood infallibility, as did the early Church. What infallibility is not is some idea made up in the nineteenth century for obscure or selfish political reasons, as is often suggested by critics. The Church sometimes proclaims doctrines and defines beliefs at various periods and at certain times but this does not imply that they did not exist beforehand or that they were just made up. Beliefs tend to be codified and outlined only when they're challenged. In other words, something considered self-evident, obvious, and extremely well-known might not be announced because it seems redundant to do so. Christ's divinity, for example, was proclaimed in AD 325 but had been accepted by His followers from His own lifetime. They accepted it to such an extent that they were willing to die for Him and His divinity only weeks after His crucifixion and would continue to be martyred in large numbers for years to come. Some may consider that they died for something that was untrue, but the point is not what we think but what they thought and they thought Christ to be the Messiah and divine. They died not for Jesus the good man, Jesus the philosopher, or Jesus the revolutionary but Jesus the Christ, the Messiah. If they were willing to make the ultimate sacrifice for this belief, it must have been an established belief, hundreds of years before it was officially codified. So the Church proclaiming something does not indicate it was not true before the proclamation and this applies to all Church teachings, including papal infallibility.

The doctrine was formally defined in 1870 at the First Vatican Council. Critics have suggested that the Pope was acting politically and to extend his own personal power, that he was some sort of isolated champion of the cause of infallibility and that most of the bishops at the council objected to the proposal. This is pure myth. Hardly any bishops objected to the doctrine – because they knew its origins and its historical and Biblical reality; it would have been a contradiction of their faith, and a denial of their position as bishops, for them to have rejected a founding doctrine of Roman Catholicism. A handful of them did have reservations for various reasons, many of those reasons being non-theological, but a more substantial 20 per cent were quite understandably concerned about the timing of the announcement and thought it might offend non-Catholics and also make life difficult for Catholics living in countries then embracing secularism and an aggressive nationalism. It was partly because of these issues of increasing concern, of course, that it was essential to remind the world of Christ and His Church, and the Pope did indeed have the authority to sometimes speak infallibly – the very nationalism and secularism spreading their influence in the 1860s and 1870s in particular in the emergent, unifying Germany would eventually be one of the major causes of the First World War and later contribute to the rise of Nazism and European fascism.[6]

Almost seventeen hundred years earlier, Irenaeus of Lyons had been challenged by not dissimilar attacks concerning the structure of the Church and had responded with "But since it would be too long to enumerate in such a volume as this the succession of all the churches, we shall confound all those who, in whatever manner, whether through self-satisfaction or vainglory, or through blindness and wicked opinion, assemble other than where it is proper, by pointing out here the successions of the bishops of the greatest and most ancient church known to all, founded and organized at Rome by the two most glorious apostles, Peter and Paul, that church which has the tradition and the faith which comes down to us after having been announced to men by the apostles. With that church, because of its superior origin, all the churches must agree, that is, all the faithful in the whole world, and it is in her that the faithful everywhere have maintained the apostolic tradition."[7]

Most of the objections to papal infallibility, however, are

not based on an informed or even uninformed criticism of the history, logic, and consistency of the belief itself but are motivated by an opposition simply to what the Pope believes and teaches about a whole collection of controversial issues. The disagreements are actually seldom if ever on issues declared by the Pope when speaking *ex cathedra,* but infallibility is used to make the papacy and Church appear absurd or anachronistic.

It's odd that when Popes have in recent years declared their concerns about, for example, wars in Iraq, Third World poverty, or the death penalty – all impossible to be matters of faith and morals and *ex cathedra* – the tired old argument about papal infallibility is not heard at all. Yet when Popes speak about, for example, the rights of the unborn or the sanctity of marriage, there is always someone around willing to throw in an infallibility reference. This is unquestionably, if not infallibly, true.

A more serious criticism is sometimes heard from non-Catholic Christians who mention the case of Honorius I, a Pope of the early seventh century. The claim is that he believed in and, more significantly, taught Monothelitism. This heresy had developed in Syria and Armenia and proposed that Jesus had only one nature, a human nature, as opposed to the orthodox Christian belief that He had two, divine as well as human. The Monophysite heresy had been condemned at the Council of Chalcedon in AD 451. It led to bitter divisions within the Church, as many refused to accept the decision and broke away. In the early seventh century, the Emperor Heraclius proposed a compromise, saying that Christ had two natures, but only one will (Monothelitism). In a letter answering a query about this, Pope Honorius seemed to say that there was only one will in Christ. He meant, however, that the human and divine wills of Christ were never in conflict. If there are two natures, there must be two wills. Monothelitism was also condemned as heretical. It strikes at the very heart of Christian belief, and if a Pope had indeed proclaimed this *ex cathedra* it would have been difficult if not impossible to explain. Catholics believe that under the guidance of the Holy Spirit, no Pope could do such a thing, not because he would be reluctant to do so but because he would be unable to do so. The problem for critics of infallibility is that while Honorius may have been one of those bad Popes – indecisive, political, opportunistic, unwise – he never made a decision on Monothelitism, let alone declared it a dogma of the Church. The example of weak Popes is more an argument in favour of than against infallibility. However flawed they may have been, these bad or unimpressive Popes never allowed the Church to teach error and never led Catholics astray. Ignatius of Antioch, as early as AD 110 in his letter to the church in Smyrna, stated: "Wherever the bishop appears, let the people be there; just as wherever Jesus Christ is, there is the Catholic Church."[8] If we look at this from a more practical standpoint, it would have been foolish if not positively cruel for Jesus to have left His followers with no guidance at all but merely a handful of men and women who saw and heard Him, weren't entirely clear on everything He taught, and thought that maybe starting a church and converting the world was a nice idea. It's preposterous. It also insults the notion of Jesus as God and God as loving us and wanting us to be taken care of. The New Testament came along later and was given to Christians by the Church, not by Christians to the Church and not by Jesus to anyone. Christ did not leave anything in writing even though He easily could have. So is it likely that He would have abandoned those He loved so much to the whims and winds of the increasingly hostile world and not left behind someone to teach and guide?

Which brings us to the Bible itself, to where it comes from and to who gave it to us. Catholics are usually accused by non-Christians of being too reliant on the Bible and often by some evangelical Christians of not using the Bible enough. In fact, the Bible is central and essential to Catholicism, but, as we've seen, the Church comes first because the Church came first. There is no Bible without the Church because it was the Church that assembled and accepted the Bible as we know it and gave it to the world. The Scriptures clearly acknowledge that they alone can never be sufficient for Christians – the Gospel of John states, "Many other signs also did Jesus . . . which are not written" and in Acts, "Then Philip ran up to the chariot and heard the man reading Isaiah the prophet. 'Do you understand what you are reading?' Philip asked. 'How can I,' he said, 'unless someone explains it to me?'"

The Bible never states that it is the sole source of Christian truth and, of course, only the Old Testament existed in anything like its totality for the first centuries of Christianity. Before one page of the New Testament was written, the Church gathered and celebrated the Eucharist, and it was in deciding which of the writings were to be used at the Mass (not which were the best for "Bible study") that the Church leaders put together a list of books – the canon. The canon as we know it was compiled by the Roman Catholic Church at Hippo in AD 393, Carthage in AD 397, and then given final approval in Rome in AD 419. All sorts of books, letters, and alternative gospels such as the Epistle of Clement, the Shepherd of Hermas, the Epistle of Barnabas, Paul's Epistle to the Laodiceans, the Preaching of Peter, and the Gospels of the Egyptians and of the Hebrews were rejected as not being inspired; the Bible we see today is what the Roman Catholic Church assembled and gave to us more than sixteen hundred years ago.[9] One has to ask those who hold the Bible to be "infallible" how they could refuse to believe in the instrument that God used to write and select this Bible – the Catholic Church?

It's worth briefly discussing at this point the allegation, usually from people who haven't read it or even looked at it in years, that the Bible is full of contradictions and that the Gospel accounts of the life of Christ are all radically different from one another, proving that they're not reliable and that the story of Jesus is not historically accurate. Reason and not faith should lead anyone with an open mind rather than an empty head to realize the inherent contradictions of this argument. The Bible did not drop from the sky but was, as we've seen, assembled by people who believed in Christ, people who were, yes, Christians – people who wanted to spread the truth of the Church and Christianity and win arguments against non-Christians and anti-Christians. Why, then, would they choose to accept and include accounts of the life of their Messiah that contradicted one another? Far better to accept only those that were entirely consistent with each other and made the pro-Christian argument that much easier. There were, after all, many other books on offer, and some of them were far more supportive of Jesus as the Messiah and contained more miraculous acts and examples and evidence of Jesus being the Son of God. The reason that some books were accepted and others not is that the Church was prepared to admit into the canon only works that were certainly inspired and certainly written by men who were present during Christ's ministry or had solid knowledge of what happened from others who were present. As for essential contradictions, there are none. There are differences in emphasis and even slight differences in interpretation because they were written by different people from different backgrounds with different literary styles who were writing for different audiences, just as four biographies may cover various aspects of a life with more or less enthusiasm and attention. The argument about Biblical contradictions is itself contradictory.[10]

The *Catholic Encyclopaedia* explains the place of the Bible in the following way: "In interpreting the Bible scientifically, its twofold character must always be kept in view: It is a divine book, in so far as it has God for its author, it is a human book, in so far as it is written by men for men. In its human character the Bible is subject to the same rules of interpretation as profane books but in its Divine character it is given into the custody of the Church to be kept and explained, so that it needs special rules of hermeneutics."[11]

This is in many ways an in-house debate among Christians and one that requires a good deal of mutual respect. Catholics fully appreciate the importance of the Bible, and they certainly believe it to be true and to be the word of God. What they question is whether as Christian individuals we have the ability to understand all of what the Bible says without the help of those ordained by God to interpret it for us. It's not an issue of the Bible not being for everyone – because it is – but about being understood by everyone. The mere possession of a Bible or an ability to read its words is surely not as important as our knowledge of what it actually means. Some of it is straightforward but much of it is complex and difficult. Even what appears easy may not be and if it really was as obvious as all that we would not have thousands of Protestant books of Biblical interpretation, Biblical reference books, and sermons by preachers explaining Biblical passages.

It's been said that the role of the Church or Magisterium as interpreter is anti-egalitarian and prevents ordinary people from having first-hand access to the word of God. On the contrary, the Church as our guide to scripture guarantees that there is equal access to Biblical truth, as opposed to an individual interpretation approach that means those with greater literary, historical, linguistic, or theological skills are assumed to have greater understanding and control over God's word than those who may be less educated or have less time to study.

Before Europe enjoyed something approaching universal literacy and before books could be produced in large numbers and at prices affordable to the masses, the Church used almost every method possible to spread the contents of the Bible and its meaning to the people. The phenomenon of the Mystery and Passion plays spread throughout the continent – and were later often banned or strictly controlled by Protestant governments – in an attempt by drama and story to explain what the Bible said and meant. Similarly in churches there were rows of pictures and carvings illustrating scripture so that people who could not read could still understand the themes contained in the written words of the Bible. Priests and itinerant preachers would explain what the Bible said, and Bibles themselves were available to those who could read them – the teaching of reading and writing and the spread of literacy were almost exclusively a Church-led initiative. One telling example of the irony and sheer ignorance of anti-Catholic attacks in this regard involves the accusation that Bibles were chained to church pews by the Catholic authorities in their churches. They were. But so were books in universities and libraries. A Bible took a very long time and a very great deal of money to compile and, as Catholics know and teach, people are sinners and one sadly common sin is theft. If Bibles had been left in churches without any security, they would have been stolen and then sold to wealthy people and so be available to only a few rather than to the many.[12]

There is a fundamental difference between the Church's role as a spiritual guide to the Bible and the censorship of literature for the sake of state control. The former is in obedience to God and is an attempt to widen and spread the truth, the latter a campaign to exert individual or government dominance over something that is considered dangerous or threatening to that individual or government. The Church ordered translations of scripture from the earliest days – the Latin Bible that was the most available version for so many centuries was originally translated into Latin because Latin was the most common, universal tongue. The Roman Catholic Church also had the Bible translated into vernacular languages, and the claim that it was Protestants rather than Catholics who first translated the Bible into English, French, and Spanish is just plain wrong. The Catholic Church sponsored and oversaw translations but refused to allow people to mistranslate scripture for their own political and religious ends. It was error and not access that the Church feared. If the Bible is the word of God, as Christians believe, it is essential to maintain it as the correct word of God and not allow it to become the word of a particular activist with a particular agenda. This is important today in an age of mass literacy when people can read various translations and at least have an opportunity to see when mistranslations have occurred, but imagine how vital it was before most people could read and write. They could be told lies, fed false information, taken away from the truth of the Bible toward the opinion of a Bible translator. This is what occurred with some of the pre-Reformation and Reformation translations, such as with the work of the English theologian William Tyndale. Tyndale may have had a lyrical turn of phrase and a genius for languages, but he also insisted on inserting his own words into passages with the specific purpose of changing their meaning. The word *congregation*, for example, was used instead of *Church*, the word *ordinance* instead of *tradition*, and instead of the original "Little children, keep yourselves from idols," he used the word *images*. The intent was quite clear: to contradict Catholic teaching even though the original words supported the Catholic position – they could not do otherwise because the Catholic position came from the text and not the other way round.[13]

In 1408 in Europe a law was passed that forbade unauthorized translations of the Bible. The law was a direct response to the translations of the English academic John Wyclif. Wycliff was an esteemed intellectual with powerful friends and patrons who instead of drawing conclusions from his studies of scripture first formed ideas about Christianity and then translated scripture in an attempt to prove his ideas. This was hardly sound scholarship, and it was irresponsible, dangerous theology. Today we have environmental bibles, feminist bibles, homosexual bibles, socialist bibles, inclusive bibles, mothers' bibles, kids' bibles, a thunderstorm of translations. It doesn't seem to have led to a more Christian and Bible-believing world.

Mind you, there is also a mass ignorance of the Mass, even among Catholics. The Mass is the epicentre of Catholic belief, but it's likely that many practising Catholics, let alone those outside of the Church, do not really understand the Mass's meaning or importance. If they did, they'd probably approach it with a lot more reverence and wonder. The actual word comes from the Latin word for *dismiss,* used at the end of the service. From earliest times, the Mass ended with "Ite, missa est" or "Go, it is the dismissal" or "Go, you have been sent." In the early church, the Mass was held in secret and those caught attending were often arrested, fined, and even tortured and executed. The Roman pagans thought they were acting as civilized people – as so many oppressors do – but in this case one of the specific reasons for their behaviour was that they had been told the Mass was cannibalism. Christians were, it was said, eating the flesh of their god and drinking his blood. The persecutors of the Christians clearly believed in the ceremony even if today so many people doubt it.[14]

The word *transubstantiation* means the change of the substance of the bread and wine on the altar into the body and blood of Jesus Christ in the Eucharist, even though all that is accessible to the senses remains as before. The earliest known use of the term was as late as the beginning of the twelfth century, and this fact has been used either unscrupulously or stupidly to argue that the doctrine itself is also medieval. It's just not so. The word is a technical term that grew out of medieval scholastic philosophy to better explain a truth of the faith that is clearly Biblical and had been held by Christians from the very beginning of the Church. The word itself may not used in the Bible – although the teaching most certainly is – but then the word *Trinity* is not used in the Bible either. It was Justin Martyr in AD 155 who first publicly outlined the Mass in his First Apology. He explained that the Mass was crucial to Christian life, was celebrated by all Christians, and unified the entire Church. The Mass, he said, is in two parts. The first was the liturgy of the word: "And on the day called Sunday, all who live in cities or in the country gather together to one place, and the memoirs of the apostles or the writings of the prophets are read, as long as time permits; then, when the reader has ceased, the presider verbally instructs, and exhorts to the imitation of these good things. Then we all rise together and pray, and, as we before said, when our prayer is ended."

The second part was the liturgy of the Eucharist: "Bread and wine and water are brought, and the presider in like manner offers prayers and thanksgivings, according to his ability, and the people assent, saying Amen; and there is a distribution to each, and a participation of that over which thanks have been given, and to those who are absent a portion is sent by the deacons."

The Didache is essential to any understanding of the early Church. It was written not only before the New Testament was compiled but before some of the New Testament was even written. It describes the workings of the earliest of Christian communities, during the first century and at a time when the Christian Church was composed of men and women who had direct experience of those who had known Jesus while He lived. It is an unparalleled guide to how the early Church functioned – in an entirely Catholic manner – and it is quite explicit concerning the Eucharist and the Mass. "Assemble on the Lord's Day, and break bread and offer the Eucharist; but first make confession of your faults, so that your sacrifice may be a pure one. Anyone who has a difference with his fellow is not to take part with you until they have been reconciled, so as to avoid any profanation of your sacrifice. For this is the offering of which the Lord has said, 'Everywhere and always bring me a sacrifice that is undefiled, for I am a great king, says the Lord, and my name is the wonder of nations.'" St. Ignatius of Antioch died in the first years of the second century, was a disciple of St. Peter and St. John, and died as a martyr when he was thrown to lions. He wrote, "But look at the men who have those perverted notions about the grace of Jesus Christ which has come down to us, and see how contrary to the mind of God they are. . . . They even abstain from the Eucharist and from the public prayers, because they will not admit that the Eucharist is the self-same body of our Savior Jesus Christ which flesh suffered for our sins, and which the Father of His goodness raised up again."[15]

Many Christians outside of the Roman Catholic Church now reject the Real Presence of Christ in the Eucharist but may not realize how recent this rejection of the Real Presence is and how vital and unchallenged the Mass was in the early Church. The belief in the Real Presence was so taken for granted by the Early Church that they did not bother to include it in the creeds that clarified teachings that had been denied by heretics — indeed, Christians argued that Jesus Christ was fully human and divine on the basis that the Eucharist was both bread and the body and blood, soul and divinity of Christ. It's hardly surprising that it was unchallenged for so long in that the teaching comes directly from scripture and from the mouth of Christ. In the synagogue at Capernaum on the shore of the Sea of Galilee, the Jewish followers of Jesus asked Him for a sign that would enable them to fully believe in Him and His teaching. They referred to their history and how under Moses, when the Hebrews were fleeing the Egyptians and were hungry in the desert, a miracle occurred and manna suddenly appeared to feed them. Jesus replied that the real heavenly bread comes from God, and when His followers asked for this bread He told them what He meant. "I am the bread of life," He explained, and "whoever comes to me will never hunger, and whoever believes in me will never thirst." At this point, His Jewish followers understood Him to be speaking metaphorically. What must also be understood is that these were devout Jews, and the Jewish teaching on dietary laws, let alone the very idea of the consumption of human flesh, were absolute and severe. Yet

Jesus went on: "I am the living bread which came down from heaven; if any one eats of this bread, he will live forever; and the bread which I shall give for the life of the world is my flesh." The reaction of Jesus' followers is significant here and cannot be dismissed. They began to argue and wonder about what they had heard. They do not simply think this another parable. They had no option when He once again repeated the phrase but this time with even more insistence. "Truly, truly, I say to you, unless you eat the flesh of the Son of man and drink his blood, you have no life in you; he who eats my flesh and drinks my blood has eternal life, and I will raise him up at the last day. For my flesh is food indeed, and my blood is drink indeed. He who eats my flesh and drinks my blood abides in me, and I in him."

This repetition is unique in the teachings of Jesus and obviously done for a purpose – one of the most significant elements of Christian belief is here declared and explained by Christ Himself so that we understand exactly what He meant. Yet so many Christians, so many of those who faithfully believe in the literal truth of scripture are suddenly convinced that when Jesus tells us about the Eucharist the truth is less literal and Christ suddenly at His most figurative. This position really doesn't make any sense at all. In other passages of the Bible, Jesus clarifies a statement if it seems to be misunderstood but here rather than using a different language or being less direct he repeats it with ever more direct language. Me, bread, blood, eat, flesh. Indeed, the Greek word that is used here for *eats* is *trogon* and means to *chew* or *gnaw* and is as literal and aggressive as it could be. There are other, softer and far more symbolic, terms that could have been used here by Jesus, terms that He frequently did employ when being metaphorical rather than literal. The disciples understood the absolute nature and reality of what was being said because some of them were terrified by the statement and its implications. "Many of his disciples, when they heard it, said, 'This is a hard saying; who can listen to it?'"

It certainly was a hard saying and it still is. Today many people refuse to accept transubstantiation just as they refused two thousand years ago – "After this, many of his disciples drew back and no longer went about with him" – but just because something is challenging and complex does not mean it is untrue. There are millions of good Christian men and women who would never doubt the virgin birth of Jesus, the miracles He performed, or the fact of His resurrection but for some reason think the transformation of bread and wine into body and blood is impossible. Their disbelief is perhaps understandable if regrettable but their argument is a thin one. Jesus was, it is said, not referring to actual physical food and wine but to spiritual nourishment. The entire speech about bread to body that is repeated so many times, runs their argument, is not about an actual act but symbolizes faith in Jesus and belief in His divinity. Why, then, would He not have made this clear when His disciples asked him to explain? It would have been callous, almost mocking, to leave them with such a false understanding, and if Jesus was callous and mocking He was not perfect and without sin and thus not the Messiah. Which is pretty damning, in every sense of the term. The words had genuine meaning – remember, Jesus was born in Bethlehem, literally "house of bread" – and these words had a particularly special meaning for Jews in first-century Palestine. *To eat flesh and drink blood* was a violent phrase meaning to hurt someone either physically or by verbal abuse. The metaphorical use of eat flesh and drink blood was negative, used by people in heated argument or even in a physical fight. So the extended logic of the metaphor argument is that Jesus, using the vernacular of the time, was telling His closest followers that they were saved and had eternal life with Him if they threatened to hurt and abuse Him. It doesn't make any sense now and it certainly wouldn't have made any sense then, which is why it wasn't used in such a way and could not have been. The context is entirely wrong, the application is anachronistic, and the meaning is lost.[16]

Christ quite clearly did use phrases such as "I am the door" and "I am the true vine" at various times in His ministry; however, they are obvious and unavoidable symbols in that He was describing Himself as the door to paradise and a vine through which we obtain spiritual sustenance. Bread can feed a person, but blood is hardly a usual means of quenching thirst, and to the Jews, drinking blood would be an unpardonable act, an anathema. Jesus insists that His followers eat, chew his flesh, something radically different from using a gentle and appropriate metaphor of a door or a vine. The most common Biblical passage quoted by critics of the Eucharist is from John, after Jesus speaks of the bread and wine and blood and body. "It is the spirit that gives life, the flesh is of no avail; the words that I have spoken to you are spirit and life." What is being explained here, some Protestant critics argue, is that even though He has just spent some time stressing the absolute importance of transubstantiation, there is actually no point in eating the bread as body and drinking the wine as blood. Not so, not so at all. Jesus isn't speaking about the Eucharist but about something else entirely. As is evident from the immediately preceding verse, he is speaking about his forthcoming ascension into heaven and about our need of the Holy Spirit in order to believe. Hence, even though one may witness in the flesh miracles and even the ascension, one needs the grace of the Holy Spirit in order

to believe. The apostle Paul would later write, "Therefore whoever eats the bread and drinks the cup of the Lord unworthily
will have to answer for the body and blood of the Lord. . . . For
any one who eats and drinks without discerning the body, eats
and drinks judgment on himself." This statement needs to be
considered carefully. Paul chose his words wisely and devoted
his life to teaching and spreading the authentic faith of Christ.
Here he didn't just recommend the Mass but emphasized not
just its importance but how dangerous it is to participate in the
Eucharist and not fully believe in it. Again, if it was merely a
passing symbol or a lyrical metaphor used as a teaching tool
this would not matter. Because it is the eternal way of being fed
with the very body of Christ it matters a great deal and, says
Paul, to accept it without understanding it and without merit is
far worse than not participating at all.[17]

Does the bread and wine become flesh and blood when
the Mass is said? There are all sorts of miracles connected to the
Eucharist, but the chances are that some scientific experiment
on a consecrated host would not reveal a protein rather than
a carbohydrate and not prove a physical transformation. It is a
mystery, a great mystery, just as was the twin nature of Christ
as God and man. Its authenticity is proved by its foundation
and by He who founded it. Some non-Catholic Christians argue
that not only is the Mass post-Biblical and even non-Christian
but that it's also a great sin because it constitutes a constant and
repeated new sacrifice of Jesus when He died once and needed
to die only once for all our sins. Indeed, He did die for the sins
of the world, once and once only. The Mass, however, is not a
new sacrifice but a participation "in spirit and in truth" in the
one and only sacrifice of Christ. It's a gift beyond our full and
complete understanding that He left us the opportunity to be

part of the Mass and part of Him for all time and in all places. The relationship with Him and the love for Him does not begin again at every Mass after somehow stopping at the end of the last one. I, for example, try to tell my wife every day I love her. This doesn't mean that I start my relationship with her anew on a daily basis or that each time I tell her I love her it is part of a fresh, original act of commitment. It's part of the same love affair with the same person. Also, when I fail her as a loving husband I try to apologise as quickly as possible. No, this isn't some cheap Valentine's Day slogan about love being something to do with never having to say you're sorry – anyone who thinks that has never been married – but true love is bound up with forgiveness, understanding, and compassion.

Which brings us to another great, grand sacrament, that of confession. The Didache again: "Confess your sins in church, and do not go up to your prayer with an evil conscience. This is the way of life. . . . On the Lord's Day gather together, break bread, and give thanks, after confessing your transgressions so that your sacrifice may be pure." Confession or reconciliation may come from God but it is the most human of sacraments, fully understanding our broken condition and our human nature. In that we are creatures made by God, this aspect of the sacrament should come as no surprise, but there is still something humbling and moving about the complete forgiveness and cleansing that takes place when someone confesses sins to God through a priest, is given gentle advice and counsel, asked to perform what is usually a mild penance, and then given absolution.

Confession is not a substitute for any other form of confession, contrition, or apologizing to God – Catholics make public confession at every Mass as part of the ceremony and are called to lead a good and moral life and ask forgiveness of

God and those around them. Confession is certainly not some spiritual or supernatural excuse that allows Catholics to behave badly, not some easy way out that opens the door of forgiveness by the mere mumbling of a few formal words so that someone can automatically be absolved and forgiven. There exists a myth that confession allows and even encourages Catholics to behave worse than they otherwise would because they can ask and be granted forgiveness at will. This myth assumes that confession is mechanical and meaningless. If it was, why would such cynical people bother with it in the first place? Confession is a direct communication with God conducted vicariously through a priest, and if the person in the confessional is prepared to lie, to apologize without meaning it, and to have no intention of trying not to repeat his offence, that is his decision. He is lying to God and, if Christianity has any meaning at all, such an action involves profound consequences. It's perverse to think that someone with so little regard for the teaching of the Church would so abuse the sacraments and have so little respect for them but if such people do exist – and surely some do – there is not very much on earth that can be done. This behaviour says a great deal about the person and absolutely nothing about the sacrament of confession. A man may abuse his wife but that doesn't mean the concept of marriage is bankrupt.

What confession does provide for the vast majority of Catholics is a conduit back to a clear relationship with God. It is humbling, sometimes even humiliating, to announce to another person one's most secret and embarrassing failings, to ask forgiveness and promise to try harder and do better. This may seem an incredibly unusual, almost shocking, approach in an age where every failing is the fault of someone else, whether it be the family, the state, the church, God, or just circumstance.

Confession does not guarantee that the sins confessed will not be repeated. Frankly, it's probably quite likely that many of them will because, God knows, sin tends to be habitual. Quite so. God knows.

But what gives a priest the right to hear a confession, let alone forgive sins? After His resurrection, Christ tells the apostles, "As the Father has sent me, even so I send you." He then breathed on them, and the only place in scripture where God breathes is when the world is created. After this Jesus tells them, "Receive the Holy Spirit. If you forgive the sins of any, they are forgiven; if you retain the sins of any, they are retained." Which is precisely what the apostles and their successors, Roman Catholic priests, did and do. It's been suggested that the sacrament was a medieval invention – the tired, predictable attack from anti-Catholics who don't seem to understand history or the Bible – because in 1215 at the Fourth Lateran Council, the Church issued a formal reminder that Catholics had to make confession at least once a year. They were merely reiterating to people what was right, and there are dozens of examples in early Christian writings of the place of confession in the Church. In AD 203, for example, Tertullian wrote regarding the sacrament that some people "flee from this work as being an exposure of themselves, or they put it off from day to day. I presume they are more mindful of modesty than of salvation, like those who contract a disease in the more shameful parts of the body and shun making themselves known to the physicians; and thus they perish along with their own bashfulness." The Church father and patriarch of Constantinople, St. John Chrysostom, wrote in the late fourth century, "Priests have received a power which God has given neither to angels nor to archangels. It was said to them: 'Whatsoever you shall bind on earth shall be bound in heaven; and whatsoever you shall loose, shall be loosed.' Temporal rulers have indeed the power of binding; but they can only bind the body. Priests, in contrast, can bind with a bond which pertains to the soul itself and transcends the very heavens. Did [God] not give them all the powers of heaven? 'Whose sins you shall forgive,' he says, 'they are forgiven them; whose sins you shall retain, they are retained.' What greater power is there than this? The Father has given all judgment to the Son. And now I see the Son placing all this power in the hands of men."[18]

Sin itself is almost unmentionable today. Even in many churches, it is more common to hear sermons about self-esteem or recycling than sin and the need to reform. One of the meanings of the word is "to miss the mark" and the word *sin* was used in ancient Greece during archery contests. "You've missed!" Sin misses the mark and tends to harm other people. The defence that if something doesn't hurt anyone it doesn't matter is usually false because someone is always harmed at some point by sin either directly or indirectly. Beyond this it also either damages or completely blocks the relationship between us and God. At the root of most sin is pride, the greatest sin of all. I know better, I know best, it's what I want. For Catholics, this sin of pride goes back to the beginning of the world and was produced by doubt. Eve knows precisely what God has told her but is persuaded by Satan to doubt that God had the authority to tell her what to do. He may have given you so much and made you so happy, says the devil, but this one command He has made is outrageous. Don't believe what He said, you know better than Him, and you should put your own opinion and desire before anything else. There's nothing original about sin apart from original sin. Problem is, it's tempting by nature and so can be difficult to resist. Men do not commit adultery because women are repulsive, people do not lie because lying makes life so difficult, thieves don't steal what isn't their property because it's unrewarding. We miss the mark because it's easy to do, and yet sin also makes it much more difficult to know God, who made us to love Him, be loved by Him, and to return to Him for eternity. Confession always brings us back, and it's there not to punish us and not to make us feel guilty but to show God's love and understanding of us and His constant willingness to give us another chance.

That return to God requires faith in Jesus Christ. Through Him it is guaranteed. It may, however, involve a waiting period on the way. It's what is known as purgatory, and purgatory tends to confuse and frighten people. It's not a place where Catholics hang around being teased by nasty ghouls in red tights, judged, and given a good telling off. It's not a halfway house used to test Christians before a final judgment is made or a place where people discover whether or not they've made it to heaven. Purgatory means *purging,* and if we're already there we're certainly going to meet God but first we need to be cleaned up a little. We qualify for paradise, but that doesn't mean we're free of sin and pride and the usual dust and dirt that surrounds human existence. The Catholic catechism puts it like this: "All who die in God's grace and friendship, but still imperfectly purified, are indeed assured of their eternal salvation; but after death they undergo purification, so as to achieve the holiness necessary to enter the joy of heaven." And "The Church gives the name Purgatory to this final purification of the elect, which is entirely different from the punishment of the damned."

It is, if you like, the place just in front of the front door. You come home from a cold, snowy night and there is the warm house, the lights on, the welcome of comfort and safety. But your boots are filthy and you're soaking wet. There is a cleaning before you enter, a drying off or a wiping of the feet. You're home, you're definitely going in but before you do you need to sort yourself out. The Letter to the Hebrews says, "Make every effort to live in peace with all men and to be holy; without holiness no one will see the Lord." We try to be holy but surely nobody sincerely believes they are holy by God's standard. Such arrogance and self-assurance is sinful in itself and will require some purging. Can you imagine a greater contrast than between the pure love with which God loves us and the faltering, mark-missing love we return? What a purifying meeting that will be when these two lovers, God and us, meet. So the Bible tells us we need more holiness before we meet with God. St. Paul writes, "But now having been freed from sin and enslaved to God, you derive your benefit, resulting in sanctification, and the outcome, eternal life." First sins are forgiven, then we are made holy or sanctified, and then we enter heaven. It's perhaps not as tempting or cozy as the thought that a Christian at death goes straight to heaven but it's far more consistent with our nature and God's plan for us. Nor should we be frightened by the concept – what we think of as suffering on earth has a different meaning in the eternal, and a bath is only intimidating to someone far too fond of being dirty to want to have a good wash.

Saints might have it a little easier but they aren't common. If they were they wouldn't be saints. Catholics acknowledge saints but worship only God. Actually, the semantics are difficult because the word *worship* has changed its meaning over the centuries. It has to be emphasized that the Church allows adoration or worship only of God and nobody else. Catholics, however, do "venerate" saints – the word comes from the word for *love* (actually the goddess of love, Venus) – and means that Catholics lovingly honour saints just as all sorts of people lovingly honour all sorts of people. Or perhaps not as all sorts of people honour all sorts of people because Catholics honour saints with the specific and grand praise they deserve. We honour their relationship with God, try to imitate their holy lives, and are inspired by their devotion and, sometimes, martyrdom. Kenneth Woodward in his book *Making Saints* sums it up rather well when he writes, "A saint is always someone through whom we catch a glimpse of what God is like – and of what we are called to be."[19] Thus Catholics also pray not so much to the saints as with them. Why would they not? It's common to hear non-Catholic Christians asking people to pray for them or offering their prayers for another person; if another person can intervene on our behalf to God, how privileged we are to be able to ask the saints in heaven to intervene for us. Saints are not statues and Catholics do not pray to inanimate objects, painted replicas of people, or anything similar. Although some Catholics may have particular devotions to particular saints and might, it is true, show too much enthusiasm to some statue or picture, they do so in spite of and not because of Catholic teaching. A statue is merely an aid to prayer, reminding us of what a great champion of the faith looked like. A man may have a photograph of his wife on his office desk but it is not his wife, a Christian may have a Bible in his hands but when he prays it is not to the Bible but to the person who the Bible is ultimately about.

Saints were honoured as early as the first century, but in the early Church there was no central structure for accepting someone's sainthood. Today the process begins locally and eventually arrives at the Holy See's Congregation for the Causes of the Saints in Rome, where someone's life and work is investigated. If this Congregation accepts the evidence, the person is declared venerable (remember, veneration means worthy of loving honour in a public way). If the Congregation for the Causes of the Saints accepts the evidence, the person is declared venerable. If they have been martyred for the sake of the faith, evidence of a miracle through their intercession is not required but otherwise miracles are required to be proved, and a selection of theologians, experts, and doctors will explore the case to decide whether the candidate may be beatified. The Church does not make someone a saint but accepts and confirms them as a saint – their life and faith made them saintly and the Church is merely admitting, after a careful examination, what is true. If any Catholic has allowed a fondness for a saint, no matter how extraordinary, to obscure, cloud, or, worst of all, block their relationship with God, neither the saint nor God will be honoured and the entire point would be lost. Saints are examples to us – St. Paul says, "A great cloud of witnesses." Saints are people who have lived out their vows of baptism to the fullest degree possible and so are named by the Church as role models, inspirations for the rest of us trying to carve out a Christian life in a deeply challenging world. They are not the passing, transitory icons of popular celebrity and media propaganda but men and women who did all and gave all for the Christian faith.

Saints are to be honoured, and so is Mary, the Mother of God. Not the Mother of God the Father or the Mother of God the Holy Spirit but the Mother of God the son – who is Jesus Christ and who had a mother. Mary was chosen by God above all others to be the earthly mother of the Messiah, the vehicle and vessel through which and from whom the saviour of the world would be delivered. Strange to think that God would have chosen just any woman to do this. Not just strange but incredible, ridiculous, a slander not as much against Mary as against God. The implication is that the creator of the world was not able to make a perfect choice. It's far more sensible and reasonable to assume that He would choose someone who was special, different, the finest of humanity, sinless. Which is why Catholics believe that we should listen to what our mother tells us. And what she tells us is essentially what Mary told the servants at the Marriage Feast at Cana: "Do whatever He tells you." So we listen, not because she is anything more than a human but precisely because she is human, the fullest and best human and the most human of us all. She is the most human because of her relationship with God – our humanity is at its finest and purest when we listen to God and love Him completely, and nobody personifies this listening and loving more startlingly than Mary. Just as with the saints, honour is due to those whose love of God reaches heroic proportions when they love Him and love His creatures. Mary has a special place in Catholicism due to her abundance of humanity. Her role is important only in how it relates to Christ, and the respect we show her is about Christ – unless we worship and believe in God the son, Jesus Christ, we have no view of Mary whatsoever. So honour of Mary can come only as a consequence of worshipping. Here was a woman who said yes to the will of God and gave herself completely to His plan. The whole equation is beyond our comprehension but we can at our best perhaps catch a glimpse of the profundity of it all, and of the absolute holiness and trust of this young woman being told that the future of the whole world rests on her goodness and her willingness to love God completely.

If critics think Mary is given too much prominence today,

they should spend more time with the fathers of the Church and the earliest Christians. St. Ambrose, writing in the middle of the fourth century: "The prophet David danced before the Ark. Now what else should we say the Ark was but holy Mary? The Ark bore within it the tables of the Testament, but Mary bore the Heir of the same Testament itself. The former contained in it the Law, the latter the Gospel. The one had the voice of God, the other His Word. The Ark, indeed, was radiant within and without with the glitter of gold, but holy Mary shone within and without with the splendour of virginity. The one was adorned with earthly gold, the other with heavenly." St. Athanasius writing fifty years earlier: "Be mindful of us, most holy virgin, who after childbirth didst remain virgin; and grant to us for these small words great gifts from the riches of thy graces, O thou full of grace. Accept them as though they were true and adequate praises in thy honor; and if there is in them any virtue and any praise, we offer them as a hymn from ourselves and from all creatures to thee, full of grace, Lady, Queen, Mistress, Mother of God, and Ark of sanctification." St. Ephrem in the early fourth century: "O Virgin Mother of God, Gate of heaven, and Ark, in thee I have a secure salvation. Save me out of the pure mercy." And St. Gregory Thaumaturgus as early as the mid-200s: "The ark is verily the holy Virgin, gilded within and without, who received the treasure of universal sanctification. Arise, O Lord, from the Father's bosom, to raise up again the ruined race of our first parent."[20]

The list goes on and on. In fact, the idea that Mary was not always virgin, not the Mother of God, not enjoying a special place in God's eyes, not someone who hears our prayers is a very late concept indeed. It's fascinating, for example, to see what even the Protestant reformers thought about Mary. The great

Martin Luther, never a man to hold back on what he thought no matter whom he might offend, said: "She is rightly called not only the mother of the man, but also the Mother of God. . . . It is certain that Mary is the Mother of the real and true God" and "It is an article of faith that Mary is Mother of the Lord and still a Virgin." John Calvin was the leader of the next generation of Protestants and developed a more severe form of theology than Luther. Even so, he maintained that Mary was ever virgin, that when the Bible refers to the brothers of Jesus it means cousins – standard belief up to then and for long afterwards as we shall see – and wrote, "It cannot be denied that God in choosing and destining Mary to be the Mother of his Son, granted her the highest honour" and "To this day we cannot enjoy the blessing brought to us in Christ without thinking at the same time of that which God gave as adornment and honour to Mary, in willing her to be the mother of his only-begotten Son." The Swiss reformer Ulrich Zwingli: "I esteem immensely the Mother of God, the ever chaste, immaculate Virgin Mary" and "The more the honour and love of Christ increases among men, so much the esteem and honour given to Mary should grow" – which is both a delightful and intensely accurate Catholic approach to the entire subject.[21]

Modern objections tend to swim around the wreck of two or three issues, and one of them is the fact of Mary's perpetual virginity. That Mary was a virgin when Jesus was born – the Virgin Birth – is a fundamental of all Christian belief, and anyone who does not accept this is, quite simply, not a Christian any more than someone who rejects the fundamentals of socialist belief is a socialist or someone who believes in God is an atheist. The virgin birth itself is beyond the scope of this book – nobody has to believe unless they are a Christian and then they have no option. Catholics, however, believe not only that Mary was a virgin when she gave birth to Jesus but that she remained so for the rest of her life. This was standard Christian belief until quite recently. My wife, the mother of our four children, once said to me, "Perhaps it's difficult for a man to understand but as a woman, as a mother, if God had made me the mother of His child, the messiah, the saviour of all humanity, the idea that I would have gone on to have a sexual relationship and have more children is ridiculous, unthinkable." It's not Biblical scholarship but it's a pretty good guide to human nature. And I can only imagine what St. Joseph – most chaste spouse – would have felt about honourably living with one who conceived of the Holy Spirit.

Critics argue that the Bible contains references to the "brethren of the Lord" and therefore that Jesus had siblings. This idea brings us to the Protoevangelium of James, written probably less than sixty years after the end of Mary's life and when numerous people who knew her and whose families knew Jesus were still alive. The text explains that as Mary's birth was prophesied, her mother, St. Anne, chose her daughter to be a perpetual virgin and to serve God at the Jewish Temple. An elderly widower named Joseph who had children from his previous marriage was chosen as her guardian. So, ran the argument, Jesus did have half-brothers and sisters but Mary was always a virgin. This theory was dominant for three hundred years until Jerome realized that the language of scripture required a closer examination. Neither ancient Hebrew nor Aramaic had an actual word that meant *cousin*, he found, so for a translation to be literal it would have to use the clumsy and effectively impossible "the son of my uncle." Instead the writers of the New Testament chose a word that signified rather than meant *brother*.

The word, in fact, had an even wider usage and could describe friends, relatives, and comrades, a practice very similar to how it is used in modern English and many other languages, both in accepted form and as slang. Part of the problem occurred when the Hebrew word for brother, cousin, or relative was translated into the Greek *adelphos* – unlike the Semitic languages Greek does have separate words for brother and cousin and *adelphos* means *brother.* So the loose, vague cousins, relatives, or even comrades of Jesus suddenly became His brothers.[22]

Part of the confusion here rests on what I like to call the "Everybody who was alive during the time of the New Testament and shortly afterwards was an idiot" theory. That is, nobody knew what death looked like and they were easily fooled by people pretending to rise from the dead. They were all invincibly naïve and believed everything that looked anything like a miracle and only people in the modern world – where reality television matters more than reality and celebrities guide our way of life – truly understand human nature. Actually these were earthy, fleshy, real, life-hardened men and women who probably knew far more about human reality than we do today. The angel Gabriel appeared to Mary and explained that she would have a baby boy. Her response is extremely important in the context of her virginity. "How can this be since I have no relations with a man?" This could mean that up to that point she had not had a sexual relationship – she was a very young woman – but the belief of her contemporaries and the early church, including some of the finest minds of the time, was that the language implied that she had taken a vow to be celibate.

Various incidents in the life of Jesus also point to His being the only son of Mary. Growing up in Nazareth, He is always described as "the son of Mary" and not "a son of Mary," and there is never any indication that there are other children in the family. When the word *brother* is used to describe friends or cousins of Jesus in the New Testament, they are never once described as being sons of Mary. This is more significant than we might think. Apply some simple logic to this: Jesus is the Messiah, His mother has been chosen by God to deliver Him to the world, and we're supposed to believe that some of those mentioned are His actual brothers and sisters. Surely, then, the people who are writing the texts and telling us what happened would want to make it abundantly clear that these people were related to Jesus and were the children of Mary because, if true, it mattered very much indeed. Not only that but they themselves, the alleged siblings of Christ, would also insist on it because their maternity would be the most significant thing in their lives.[23] They would have been alive when the themes and content, if not the actual writing, of the Gospels were being moulded and confirmed. If the authors wanted to remove any trace that Jesus had siblings, they would have used another word to describe them, a word that could not possibly be thought to signify brother or sister. If they wanted to stress that He did have siblings, they would have at least once if not repeatedly used "son of Mary" as they used when speaking about Jesus. But instead they used the best word they had to describe a cousin and that word was *cousin*. Simple really and, anyway, nothing else makes any sense.

It may sound paradoxical or even ironic but Biblical interpretation and understanding require more than faith. Some readers of the Bible – for their own reasons – may want Jesus to have had siblings but this doesn't suddenly make it true. Look at the scene of the crucifixion, the description of that magnificent, majestic passage from Christ to death before resurrection. As He is dying in agony, He tells John to take care of His mother, to be with Mary and make sure she is protected. Yet the so-called brothers of Jesus are James, Joseph, Simon, and Jude. What type of person would ask someone outside of their family to look after a mother and ignore the duties, obligation, love, and devotion of the biological children of that woman? Some of those alleged brothers, especially James, were to feature quite heavily in the early Church, but none of them ask for special privileges and for any particular authority because of their relationship with Jesus and Mary – who, remember, had a special place in the Church then as she does now. It all seems so clear when we step back and look at it.

Yet still the questions continue. Remember, critics say, that in the Gospel of Matthew it is written, "And he did not know her till she brought forth her firstborn son." The implication is obvious. First, critics ask, why use the word "until" unless something occurred afterwards? Second, why use the word *firstborn* unless there were second-, third-, or fourth-born? All very neat but quite a shock to King Saul's daughter. From the second book of Samuel: "Michal the daughter of Saul had no children till the day of her death," meaning, according to the application above, that Michal had children after her death. And this usage of the word is common not only in scripture but in ancient writings in general. Words have changed meaning in two thousand years, and languages can be translated for literal accuracy or accuracy of meaning and spirit, the two approaches sometimes being mutually exclusive. In the Bible, the word *till* simply tells us something has not happened yet but has no reference to that event happening later. Even in contemporary idiom, most languages, if we consider the phrase in our minds and perhaps use a different inflection, do not necessarily consider *till* to mean that an act is inevitable afterwards. As for *firstborn*, this is just weak thinking and flabby scholarship. In the Bible, *firstborn* was the word used to describe the child that opened the womb of a mother and was used to describe any first child, whether they had siblings or not. The law of Moses, which was central to the lives of Mary and her family and her community as well as those who wrote the Bible, gave a special place to a firstborn son, who was to be sanctified and held in high esteem.

Mary was also held in high esteem, which is why the Church teaches the doctrines of the Immaculate Conception and the Assumption. The first was promulgated in 1854 and the second in 1950. And before anyone suggests that theological beliefs can't be made up almost two millennia after events actually happened, we've already outlined how beliefs are confirmed when challenged or when people need to be reminded of their authenticity and importance. I don't go around telling people I can swim, for example, or that I can ride a bike but it doesn't mean I can't swim or ride a bike because I can.

First: the Immaculate Conception, which is not the Virgin Birth. It means that Mary was conceived just like anyone else but without original sin. *Immaculate* means without stain. She was chosen by God at the point of her conception and was kept free from original sin and in a state of grace. As Catholics say in the rosary and as Luke records in the Gospel, the angel Gabriel greets Mary with "Hail, full of grace, the Lord is with you." The early Church taught that Mary was untouched by sin and this made her unique in humanity. This meant that she lived, always and forever, in perfect communion with God because it is sin that prevents us from doing this; to live in perfect communion with God is His intention or, if you like, the way it is supposed to be. But, critics argue, the Bible tells us that we are all sinners so surely Mary needs a saviour just as we all do.

That's correct. The analogy used by Catholics for centuries is that of a man who falls into a pit but is pulled out. A woman is also about to fall into the pit, but just before she falls someone pulls her back. She has been saved just as has the man but earlier and in anticipation of the fall. The man is all muddy and dirty but, in the end, is saved from the pit. The woman is not muddy or dirty because she has been saved before she even falls. Mary is not equal to God and she is not equal to Jesus; she is entirely human but entirely special. God chose her to be who and what she was. The doctrine was proclaimed by Pope Pius IX in 1854 not because it was being denied but because it was thought to be so important and so necessary that Catholics needed to be reminded of it.

The Assumption was a teaching of the Church from at least as early as the sixth century, and this belief that Mary's body did not corrupt but was immediately reunited with her soul was standard teaching more than a hundred years earlier. In the Eastern churches, it is described as the Dormition, or the Falling Asleep. The Assumption is the belief that at the end of her life Mary was assumed, body and soul, into heaven. She did not "ascend" into heaven as Jesus did but was assumed into heaven by God. It's interesting that while the early Church, and indeed the Catholic Church throughout its history, has collected and revered the remains of the saints, there was never any suggestion that Mary's body or bones existed. Not so Peter, Paul, and the writers of the Gospels but with Mary there is not a hint. Those closest to her and to her era did not challenge the notion of the Assumption and believed that as she came into the world with a startling purity so surely she would leave the world in a similarly miraculous fashion. "We pronounce, declare and define it to be a divinely revealed dogma: that the

Immaculate Mother of God, the ever Virgin Mary having completed the course of her earthly life, was assumed body and soul to heavenly glory," said Pope Pius XII in 1950. Hail Mary. Quite literally, hail Mary.

The word *rosary* comes from the Latin *rosarium*, meaning a garland of roses because the rose is one of the flowers associated with the Virgin Mary. The rosary is sometimes mistakenly thought to have been invented by St. Dominic in the late twelfth or early thirteenth century but we have evidence of the rosary or something very similar being prayed long before. The rosary is not a prayer devoted to Mary but to God, which is why in addition to the Hail Mary it contains the Apostles' Creed, the Lord's Prayer, and the Glory Be. The creed has its origins in AD 125 and the modern form came into being in the fifth century. To put it bluntly, it doesn't get much more Christian than this: "I believe in God, the Father Almighty, Creator of heaven and earth, and in Jesus Christ, His only Son, our Lord, who was conceived by the Holy Spirit, born of the Virgin Mary, suffered under Pontius Pilate, was crucified, died, and was buried. He descended into hell. The third day he arose again from the dead. He ascended into heaven and is seated at the right hand of the Father. From thence he shall come to judge the living and the dead. I believe in the Holy Spirit, the holy Catholic Church, the communion of saints, the forgiveness of sins, the resurrection of the body, and the life everlasting. Amen." The Lord's Prayer is self-explanatory. It's the prayer taught by Christ to His followers, which is why it's said in the rosary and at every Roman Catholic Mass.

The Hail Mary is said repeatedly during the rosary, and there is a perhaps understandable fear that this is a prayer to Mary and has nothing to do with God. It's an understandable error until we understand the truth. The prayer begins with words from Luke's Gospel and then "Blessed art thou among women, and blessed is the fruit of thy womb, Jesus," which is what Elizabeth, Mary's cousin, said to her. The line "Holy Mary, Mother of God, pray for us sinners, now and at the hour of our death" may not be taken directly from the Bible – as we've noted earlier, neither is the Trinity – but it's precisely in keeping with Christian thought and the beliefs of the Church from the earliest days. The Glory Be – "Glory be to the Father, and to the Son, and to the Holy Spirit. As it was in the beginning, is now, and ever shall be, world without end" – is straightforward, and the closing prayer, the Hail Holy Queen or Salve Regina, was composed in the eleventh century to honour Mary and longs for the sight of "the blessed fruit of thy womb, Jesus." The prayer is recited while meditating on the most important aspects of the life, works, teachings, and ministry of Jesus. The "mysteries," as they are known, are divided into the Joyful, Sorrowful, Glorious, and Luminous. Each one is devoted to five chapters in Jesus' life: Joyful to the Annunciation, the Visitation, the Nativity, the Presentation of Jesus at the Temple, and the finding of Jesus at the Temple; the Sorrowful to the Agony in the Garden, the Scourging at the Pillar, the Crowning with Thorns, the Carrying of the Cross, and the Crucifixion; the Glorious Mysteries, being the Resurrection, the Ascension, the Descent of the Holy Spirit, the Assumption of Mary, and the Coronation of Mary; finally, the Luminous to the Baptism of Jesus, the Wedding at Cana and the first miracle, the proclamation by Jesus of the Kingdom of God, the Transfiguration, and the Institution of the Eucharist.

Mary is asked in the prayer to intercede for us as we consider Jesus and meditate on His life, death, and resurrection, just as she interceded at Cana, so close to Nazareth and the family home, when she asked her son to change the water into wine. He listened and He obeyed, did what His mother asked of Him. Doing what is asked is at the centre of Roman Catholic theology, doing what is asked of us by God and His Son Jesus Christ. The Church is the vehicle left to us that will lead us back to God, left to us under the leadership of the Pope so that we will not be alone and left to wander with thousands of competing ideas about what a passage of the Bible might mean or not mean, and left to us to give us direction in a world ruled by fashion and subject to political, social, and moral storms. Does the Church change with the times? It understands the times and responds to them but to change with them for the sake of change would be terribly dangerous if not disastrous. God gives us free will because He is a loving God. If He had made it completely obvious that Christianity was true, He would have given us no freedom of choice and we would respond out of robotic self-interest. If He were almost impossible to find, He would be cruel, like some supreme vivisectionist watching us scurry around in a laboratory. No, He gives us just enough evidence if we make the effort to find Him. At its most visible, the evidence is in the form of the Roman Catholic Church, its teaching, and its theology and the seven sacraments – baptism, Eucharist, confession, confirmation, marriage, Holy Orders, and the anointing of the sick – that compose a series of stepping stones back across the tides to where we belong.

CATHOLICS
AND LIFE

IT'S THE SUBJECT CATHOLICS talk about a great deal and the
one that they are criticized for talking about a great deal. In
fact, they are criticized for being obsessed with the life issue,
of being monomaniacs and single-issue extremists. Actually,
such criticisms are usually nothing more than digressions or attempts to avoid the subject and dismiss the people discussing it.
We talk about issues of life and sexuality because they matter.
In a better world, the subjects we're about to discuss here would
be embraced by everybody, but, the world being what it is, it's
left to Christians and to the Roman Catholic Church in particular to take a stand and to speak up for the most vulnerable of
people – the unborn, the elderly, the ill and handicapped, the
most marginalized of marginalized. Catholics believe that life
begins at conception and ends at natural death, and we know
that this belief runs directly and increasingly contrary to the
drift of Western society. Roman Catholicism is also inherently
connected to, and an exponent of, natural law in that nature is
God-given, and the laws of nature are as immutable and real as
are the laws of gravity. It is in no way surprising that the Church
champions unborn children or those threatened by euthanasia
because nature tells us when life begins and when it ends. There
are also, however, Biblical references to the unborn – Psalm 139
has "For you created my inmost being; you knit me together
in my mother's womb. I praise you because I am fearfully and

wonderfully made; your works are wonderful, I know that full well. My frame was not hidden from you when I was made in the secret place. When I was woven together in the depths of the earth, your eyes saw my unformed body. All the days ordained for me were written in your book before one of them came to be." Job has "Did not he who made me in the womb make them? Did not the same one form us both within our mothers?" and Jeremiah, "Before I formed you in the womb I knew you, before you were born I set you apart; I appointed you as a prophet to the nations."

But the Catholic defence is as much a moral and logical one based on science and on human rights as it is a religious or scriptural argument. All rights are important but the most inalienable and the most fundamental is the right to life. In fact, no right has any meaning unless it is underpinned by the most natural and essential right and that is, of course, the right to be allowed to be born. The argument is also about love, the love that increasingly dare not speak its name, the love for the unborn.

Some basic science first. At the moment of conception, a male sperm unites with a female ovum to fertilize it, and the single-celled organism formed is called a zygote, an intricate and sophisticated repository of biological information of both parents. Fertilization occurs in the Fallopian tube, and shortly afterwards cells move to the uterine wall of the womb. Within the next twenty-four to forty-eight hours, the tiny zygote multiplies at an extraordinary rate and becomes what is called a blastocys or a placenta, containing 150 cells. This is the embryo and will last until the eighth week of development. From the eighth week until birth, the word *fetus* is used. One month after conception, the eyes, ears, and respiratory stem are developing. A week later, the heart can be felt beating, and the following week the baby can grip and bend its fingers. Eleven weeks after conception there is steady breathing and then the baby will be able to swallow the amniotic fluid. Around two weeks after this, around fourteen weeks from conception, the baby can taste, and between sixteen and twenty weeks the baby can hear, including hearing its mother's heartbeats. At twenty-three weeks after conception, the baby is sleeping regularly, and six months after conception the baby's sweat glands are functioning. The following month the baby kicks, stretches, performs somersaults. From this point on there is considerable weight gain and at around nine months the baby is born and, suddenly, has a right to life, liberty, education, and the right to free speech, health care, assembly, and whatever else.[1] It all seems rather arbitrary that these secondary rights are suddenly given to a person who up until that point had no right under law to be born and to not be killed.

At conception a child has a unique DNA and genomic character and is already unlike anyone who has been conceived or born before or anyone who will be conceived or born afterwards. It is a distinct human life and like all human life in a civilized society should have a right to exist. Yet the last twenty years have seen a curious twisting of the debate around the abortion issue and a monumentally successful campaign to marginalize pro-life opinion. Politicians are told that to even discuss the policy would lose them votes – though polls repeatedly show people at best as being divided on the subject – and opponents of abortion, whatever their views on other issues, are portrayed as wild-eyed zealots. This has made an informed, respectful discussion of the issue extremely difficult because the mere mention of abortion is enough to make many people in politics, media, and public life turn away as if their lives were threatened. Actually it's not their lives but the lives of unborn children that are in danger.[2]

The reasons for the pro-life position are many and obvious. A woman has the choice to do whatever she wants with a tuft of hair or an appendix but not with a distinct person within her. The unborn child cannot survive outside of the womb but then a fully developed newborn child, or for that matter an injured or sick adult, will die quickly if left without care. Size is the most obvious difference between an unborn child and a teenager or adult, but this is a facile observation. After three months of growth, there is no new major development in an unborn baby. At nine months, the unborn child is more mature but then a five-year-old is more mature than a two-year-old, a teenager more mature than a ten-year-old. We know instinctively that this is a child, witnessed by how we would react if we saw an obviously pregnant woman smoking or drinking. We've been programmed to think differently if we see a pregnant woman opting to end the life of her powerless child. Much of the reluctance to consider the issue is precisely because when people do study abortion beyond the hyperbole of the mistakenly and misleadingly named pro-choice argument, they become so terribly disturbed and distressed. So they'd rather be ignorant than uncomfortable.

The arguments for abortion have been heard numerous times, especially in a media that is so often devoted to the abortion cause. While those in the pro-life movement are accused of obsession, it seems to be their opponents who are truly committed, never wasting an opportunity to promote their position and to dismiss pro-life arguments. How many detective dramas have we seen, for example, where abortion doctors are killed? Such a violent action is never justified and is, thankfully and contrary to what some would have us believe, incredibly rare, but compared with the millions of children aborted in recent years, an isolated assault on an abortion doctor does rather pale in comparison. So do the arguments in favour of abortion when they're carefully considered. How about abortion, runs one of the most common debating points, in cases of rape and incest? These tragedies provide less than a fraction of 1 per cent of the reasons for abortion, and they are mentioned by abortion advocates simply to make pro-lifers appear extreme, claiming that pro-life advocates don't care about rape victims or young girls forced into sex by a father. It's nonsense, of course, but it does help win an argument. We should ask if those who support abortion in these rare cases would oppose it when rape and incest are not the causes of pregnancy. It would in most cases be a rhetorical question. Catholics believe that life is sacred and that while compassion, empathy, and understanding are essential, we cannot punish one crime by committing another. A rapist is a criminal, his child is not. Pro-abortion activists ask this question less because they care about rape and incest but more because they want to make the pro-life position appear unreasonable.

But surely if abortion is not legal and readily available, the argument continues, there will be countless deaths in back-street abortions. Actually, we have no idea how many of these atrocities took place because they were, obviously, illegal and nobody would have been so foolish as to keep detailed records. There is no doubt that back-street abortions occurred, that women were treated terribly and were exploited and sometimes died. We know for a fact, though, that women die in legal, often publicly funded front-street abortions and that babies die in hideously greater numbers now that abortion has not only been legalized but is often encouraged either indirectly by the culture or directly by the abortion industry, which is not, as some would have us believe, purely altruistic, interested only in women's health, and indifferent to profit. The problem is not where the abortion takes place but that it takes place anywhere at all. When it does, a baby is killed.

Another regular taunt is that only women have a right to comment on this issue. This is hardly a serious argument. Men are fathers, men are taxpayers, men are citizens. Men are also abortionists. Actually most abortionists are men and most of the people who profit from abortion are men. Men are also frequently responsible for abortions in that they do not fulfil their roles as fathers, abandon vulnerable women who are pregnant, and bring pressure to bear on women whom they have made pregnant because they do not want the responsibilities of fatherhood. The laws of a state are formed not only by the people whom they directly affect but by the state represented and led by the government and the judiciary for the good and protection of all people, whatever their gender, race, religion, or background. Surely it is the nature and quality of the argument rather than the gender of the individual making the argument that should inform our position. Gender bias does, however, lead to far more baby girls being aborted than baby boys. Modern technology has met with archaic gender preferences, and in parts of the Third World in particular, and in diaspora communities in Europe and North America, women are aborting babies if they are female, keeping them if they're male. Rather a bitter paradox for feminist ideology. Yet if the unborn child is genuinely nothing more than tissue with no rights, the sex of the fetus should not be an issue – strangely enough, gender-selected abortion is certainly an issue for many people who would describe themselves as pro-choice, meaning that they've been living something of an ideological lie. They may argue that the specific killing of unborn little girls is morally irrelevant but viscerally they react to it because they know abortions based on the sex of the fetus are wrong. They know they are girls, and girls being killed purely because of their sex.

Nor is this a question of choice at all. Choice implies the possibility of a positive decision – the choice to say or do something, travel somewhere, be something. The choice to kill is considered both ethically and legally not a choice at all but a transgression of a code that allows meaningful choice to others. If a killer chooses to kill, a victim loses the choice to live. The argument that someone does not approve of abortion themselves, would never have an abortion, but would not stop someone else from having an abortion makes no sense – which is why it's so often used by politicians! If abortion is not the taking of a life, it is always permissible; if it is the taking of a life, it is never permissible. The only reason to be opposed to it is if it is truly the killing of an innocent human being, and if this is so, one does not have the option of personally not wanting to kill while enabling and allowing others to do so. If it's wrong it's wrong. This is not an ethically neutral act even if so many people pretend it to be so because they fear social abuse or political defeat if they take a stand.[3]

Remember, as science and medicine advances, we will be able to preserve the lives of more and more early-term babies at earlier and earlier periods in their development. They will be able to survive outside of the womb at a very young age. Does this still mean that abortion is based on the point of independent, viable life? Not that it seems to matter very much even now because there are ghoulish cases where babies have survived abortion and been left to die. In other such cases, nurses have intervened to save the life of the baby, which raises any number of questions that in a saner scientific and ethical environment would never have to be asked.[4]

The unborn are vulnerable but the handicapped or disabled unborn even more so. We claim to be an enlightened age, more progressive and tolerant than at any time in the past and certainly more diverse and kind than the Catholic-based societies of old that we so like to use as examples of how we have evolved. We will provide facilities for handicapped people and congratulate ourselves on how we care for them. Yet abortion now deliberately targets those whose handicap can be detected in the womb, as many disabilities can be now and as many more will be in the future. Children with Down Syndrome, for example, are being aborted at a grotesque rate and there may come a time when we hardly ever see such people in society, where few if any children will even know what a Down Syndrome person looked like. On the one hand, we tell people with physical and mental challenges that they are equal and that everybody has equal worth but simultaneously we offer, allow, and sometimes encourage – it is standard for a doctor to inform a mother if an unborn baby has what is known as a "defect" and offer the grand euphemism of an "alternative to birth" – the removal of babies who may grow up looking a little different from the rest of the population.

Similar arguments apply to embryonic stem-cell research. The Catholic Church, the great promoter of science and scientific progress, is not at all opposed to stem-cell research but to the taking of cells from unborn children who cannot, obviously, give their permission. Stem cells can be taken from umbilical cords, the placenta, amniotic fluid, adult tissues and organs such as bone marrow, and fat from liposuction and regions of the nose. Stem cells can even be taken from cadavers up to twenty hours after death. There are in fact four different types of stem cell: embryonic stem cells, embryonic germ cells, umbilical cord stem cells, and adult stem cells. In that germ cells can be obtained from miscarriages that do not involve an abortion, the Church opposes only one of the three forms of stem-cell research, a position that may be surprising to some for the media has created the impression that if it were not for the Catholic Church's opposition to stem-cell research, any number of terrible diseases and illnesses would be solved almost overnight. Although enormous progress has been made with stem-cell research, there is not a case of a single person being cured through the use of embryonic cells, partly because adult stem cells are obviously part of an adult body whereas embryonic stem cells are not.[5]

But at heart it comes down to the morality of using an aborted child for medical research or creating with the use of exploitative science some sort of clone – and remember that the creation of a cloned embryo for the purpose of harvesting cells is still the initiation of life for the sole purpose of using that life. Yet some argue that as abortions already take place – and in obscenely large numbers – it is tragic to merely discard these embryos when, whether we object to abortion or not, they could be used for a noble purpose and to help humanity. These babies may be dead but to humiliate and abuse them even after death and mutilate their tiny bodies is an extra insult to a unique human being. It is also likely to encourage further abortions in poor countries with women being bribed to conceive and then abort. It's sad but true that medical science does not always allow itself to be determined by greater ethics, an example being the medical experiments conducted by the Nazis in the 1940s and some of the results obtained by the horrible exploitation of concentration camp inmates and political prisoners. Modern science has come to a consensus that any findings thus gathered cannot be used, and very few people would disagree with this. The human body possesses an innate and natural dignity, and even in death we cannot use a human body for whatever purpose without prior consent.

Once again, the Catholic Church refuses to accept a human hierarchy, whether it is based on race, gender, ability, or age. Black, white, male, female, handicapped or able-bodied, unborn, middle-aged, old, dying, or in the prime of life. No person should have immoral authority over another merely because they have the power by size, wealth, privilege, or race. It seems an eminently humanistic proposal, but when Catholicism articulates it, the Church is accused of interfering in areas that should not concern it.

Hand in hand with this move to legitimize abortion and allow the use of the aborted is the mantra we hear a great deal in the economically developed countries: that the world is overpopulated, that primarily Africa and Asia have too many people, and that as a consequence wealthy people have the right if not the duty to eliminate poor people. Actually the world is not overpopulated at all but the West is certainly greedy. We artificially divide up African regions, call them countries, and then wonder why they don't function properly. We install dictators, sell them arms, exploit their natural resources, fight our wars vicariously through them, give them the example of corrupt colonial rule, and then wonder why they are not stable and cannot feed themselves. There is one notably painful example of the different assumptions, expectations, and existences of people in the wealthy and the poor world. There is in Africa a wild-growing grass, *Hoodia gordonii,* that when sucked and chewed lessens the pains of hunger; it is given by mothers to their starving children. The grass has now been turned into capsules to be taken by obese people in the West as an appetite suppressant. The juxtaposition of one people forced by necessity to deal with terrible hunger and another by indulgence to control their inflated appetites not only is poignant but should be an embarrassment to the developed world. It's unjust, un-Catholic, and wrong. Yes, un-Catholic. Absolute equality is impossible and not even desirable, but the obscene gap between wealthy and poor in the world is outrageous and has Western politicians concluding that the solution to Third World hunger issues is to reduce the population. No, the solution is to help them and allow them to feed themselves properly. It is always agonizing to see some of the champions of the permissive society in Hollywood – dramatically and hysterically anti-Catholic – making well-publicized trips to Africa and Asia to adopt a local baby. They may mean well – though the fashion for such adoption is sickening – but what they fail to appreciate is that the solution to child poverty is not to remove the children but to remove the poverty. This is what the Catholic Church has been demanding for decades, for a radical redistribution of wealth so that all of God's creatures can enjoy the comforts of a full belly and a long life.

Nor is this hypocrisy confined to Africa. In Peru, for example, the government has great trouble feeding its people and maintaining proper levels of nutrition for its children. This seems strange in a country with a massive annual fish catch, one that should be sufficient to feed the population with healthy and vitamin-packed fish products. Up to half the catch, however, is exported to North America to be used as cat food.

The Catholic Church argues that it is not the size of the population that matters but how we treat that population. The Catholic commitment is to a world where skin colour and geographical location are less important than the Christian belief in the equal value of every human being. People do live in crowded condition but they always have, no matter how small the population. It's human nature and economic reality that we assemble close together in order to exchange goods and maintain communal life and collective safety. There is nothing new in that at all. People actually occupy around 3 per cent of the earth's land surface. If 1,200 square feet was given to every person in the world, they would still all fit into an area the size of Texas – whether the Texans would object is an altogether different issue! World population growth is also declining. United Nations figures reveal that the 79 countries that make up 40 per cent of the world's population now have fertility rates too low to prevent population decline. The rate in Asia fell from 2.4 between 1960 and 1965 to 1.5 between 1990 and 1995. In Latin America and the Caribbean, for the same dates the rates fell from 2.75 to 1.70. Europe, of course, is rapidly losing its population altogether – 0.16 between 1990 and 1995, which really means zero.[6]

In that environmentalism has taken on an almost religious fervour, it's hardly surprising that leading activists fear that "overpopulation" will damage the environment and have disastrous effects on the planet's ecological system. The worrying inconsistencies of the green movement aside, we need to remember that many if not most of the especially lovely parts of the world with the greatest environmental quality are in densely populated countries. Rain forests, for example, are not disappearing because of overpopulation. In Brazil, where some of the major damage is occurring, the population per square mile is far less than half the world average. As for air and water pollution, some of the most egregious cases of damage and poor quality have been in countries such as Poland, Russia, and China where population growth is extremely low.

The Food and Agriculture Organization of the United Nations estimates that food surpluses are close to 50 per cent in the developed world and around 17 per cent in the developing world – hardly proof that people starve because of too little food. Food supplies have doubled in the last 50 years, and farmers currently work on half the world's arable land. The food is there, if it is distributed fairly and competently. The Ethiopian famine in 1984 and 1985, for example, is a horrendous case not of people dying due to lack of food production but of a corrupt government stealing food from farmers and businessmen and selling it to buy arms. It was socialism and not overpopulation that led to the terrible suffering. Africa, in fact, has one-fifth the population density of Europe, and Taiwan, with five times the population density of mainland China, produces much more per capita than its Communist neighbour.[7]

The Church has also tried to oppose the idea that, even if overpopulation is a myth, the people of the developing world themselves want to reduce their numbers and the West should listen to them. The evidence says otherwise. There are warehouses full of condoms in Bangladesh and the Philippines where in spite of education or propaganda campaigns from the government, often via pressure from Western states, the population is simply not interested in using them. The idea of abortion is an alien concept in the Islamic world and most of Africa, and, if anything, these countries want to increase their population and deeply resent what they see as the cultural imperialism

– usually so opposed by the left – attempted by pro-abortion and socially liberal politicians from Europe and North America.[8]

So the Catholic Church and faithful Catholics show a certain commitment, even an obsession, with the saving of innocent life. It is nothing at all to be ashamed of and something that, one day, will be seen as a mark of honour – just as the early opponents of slavery or "premature" opponents of the rise of fascism are now honoured. At the time of their activism, they were regarded as extremists and troublemakers who, according to establishment wisdom, would be better off involving themselves in something that mattered. The Church, though, has always held up a mirror in which society can see reflected some of its uglier aspects, and it does not like what it sees. Thus it becomes angry but not, as it should be, with itself but with the Church. This is particularly noticeable when it comes to issues of personal gratification and sexuality and especially, apart from abortion, when issues of artificial contraception, condoms, and the birth-control pill are discussed. The Church warned in the 1960s that far from creating a more peaceful, content, and sexually fulfilled society, the universal availability of the pill and condoms would lead to the direct opposite. In the decade since, we have seen a seemingly inexorable increase in sexually transmitted diseases, so-called unwanted pregnancies, sexuality-related depression, divorce, family breakdown, pornography addiction, and general unhappiness in the field of sexual relationships. The Church's argument was that far from liberating women, contraception would enable and empower men and reduce the value and dignity of sexuality to the point of transforming what should be a loving and profound act into a mere exchange of bodily fluids. The expunging from the sexual act the possibility of procreation, the Church said, would reduce sexuality to mere self-gratification. Pleasure was vital and God-given but there was also a purpose, a glorious purpose, to sex that went far beyond the merely instant and ultimately selfish.

This also applied to the Church's attitude toward the use of condoms in Africa. When, for example, in 2009 Pope Benedict XVI made a series of comments about the dangers of condom use in Africa in the attempt to prevent AIDS, there was an outpouring of applied ignorance and proof after proof, if we needed it, of the survival of anti-Catholic prejudice. Talk-radio hosts who had long callously and naïvely blamed Africans for all of Africa's sufferings suddenly became champions of the continent. Doctors and academics who had shown no previous concern for the plight of Africa were instantly transformed into experts and partisans.

First some context. AIDS had smashed its way through Africa for almost two generations before many people in Europe or North America had even heard of it. It killed poor black people many miles away, and nobody matters less to the wealthy white than poor blacks many miles away. It was only when the disease was brought into the male homosexual community of the United States that the likes of Elizabeth Taylor became so emotional on television, and numerous actors, politicians, and public figures made it one of the most fashionable causes in modern times. AIDS was killing people just like them, and they could identify with its horror and were terrified that they could be the next to suffer. Indeed, AIDS is a fascinating case study in itself in that while politicized statistics and agenda-driven activists try to tell us otherwise, AIDS in the West is still most prevalent among gay men and intravenous drug users. The public was told in North America and elsewhere that in various areas the infection rate had doubled in the heterosexual community. This was often true. What was not always volunteered was that these were often small towns, and the numbers had increased from one person to two or two people to four. But it is the suffering itself rather than the nature of the sufferer that should motivate us. Catholicism teaches that it is a person's humanity and not their sexuality or addiction that obliges us to care for them and love them. Problem is, this philosophy was rarely applied by the secular world when it was Africans rather than Californians who were in need.

That, at least, seemed to be the attitude of many in the Western elites, who were the very people most condemning of the Roman Catholic Church when it announced that it opposed the use of condoms to deal with the AIDS crisis in Africa. Yet it was the Church that was in Africa caring for people with AIDS long before the disease was widely known in North America and Europe and when Hollywood and the Western media were more concerned with puppies and kittens. Mind you, cats and dogs still seem to concern celebrities and their public supporters more than starving children. Even today almost half of all African people with AIDS are nursed by men and women working for the Roman Catholic Church – a Church, by the way, that has also called for all African debt to be forgiven and for a radical redistribution of wealth to be instituted from the northern to the southern hemisphere.

It was highly unusual for any of this to be mentioned when Pope Benedict was attacked for his condemnation of the condom fetish. If we read the man's statements, however, what we see is a sophisticated deconstruction of Western double standards and a thoughtful critique of the failed attempt to control AIDS. First, it's not working. In countries where condoms are state-distributed, are free, and are ubiquitous, AIDS has not been controlled and is often spreading. Second, even where AIDS is less of an issue, such as in North America, the increased availability and use of condoms has coincided with an annual increase in STDS and so-called unwanted pregnancies. Third, one failure of a condom to work – and the failure rate is significant if not overwhelming – is not a mere mistake but a death sentence. Fourth, condoms enable promiscuity rather than encourage abstinence. And sexual activity is about more than mere intercourse; a cut finger or a small body wound can allow infection to occur. Fifth, how dare we treat black people and those who live in the developing world as if they were children? They are as capable of self-control as anyone else. All over Africa, most successfully but not exclusively in Uganda, there are elaborate, empathetic, and extraordinarily successful abstinence programs that emphasise humanity rather than lust – a philosophy that runs directly contrary to the sexual gratification cult so favoured by some of the people in the West who are so opposed to Church teaching of sexuality and who became so apoplectic at Pope Benedict's comments.

Of course, there is more to this anti-papal neurosis than television comedians making jokes about celibate clergy and commentators assuming that they know far more about Third World reality than a priest who has worked in an African city slum for forty years. Conventional wisdom has it that Africa has a population problem and that Africans can become "more civilized" if they have fewer children. It's an organized and sometimes quite sinister campaign. Africa is, if anything, underpopulated and the problems of the continent are far more about Western greed, colonization, resources, and arms sales than about family size. The Church has spoken out on these issues for decades and was, for example, one of the leading voices at the United Nations that persuaded the multinational pharmaceutical companies to make their early anti-AIDS drugs generic and thus affordable in the developing world.

The Catholic approach to contraception is not new, in spite of the central modern document on the subject in 1968. The encyclical *Humanae Vitae* or *On Human Life* came at a most important time in the evolution of sexual ethics. These were the 1960s, and in 1968 in particular the Western world was embracing a new, open, and what was considered liberated approach to sexuality and life. The Second Vatican Council had met, Paul VI was not considered a particularly conservative Pope, and many of those who objected to traditional Church teaching expected a new and even revolutionary approach. It was supremely naïve really but more the product of selfish wishful thinking than a genuine understanding of what Catholicism and Catholic moral order is about. As is often the case, the Church demonstrated what being truly counter-cultural meant and surprised and disappointed many people by reiterating and justifying the pristine beauty of marriage, married love, and the unworthiness and life-belittling nature of contraception. It surprised and disappointed those who were interested in change for the sake of change and not in change as a means to spread the Christian Gospel. To purposely and artificially obstruct God's plan for marriage and the creation of life was intrinsically wrong, said the encyclical, but natural family planning was permitted because it still allowed the possibility of God's plan to be fulfilled. The document stated that contraception was "any action which, either in anticipation of the conjugal act or in its accomplishment, or in the development of its natural consequences, proposes, whether as an end or as a means, to render procreation impossible." And "we must once again declare that the direct interruption of the generative process already begun, and, above all, directly willed and procured abortion, even if for therapeutic reasons, are to be absolutely excluded as licit means of regulating birth. Equally to be excluded, as the teaching authority of the Church has frequently declared, is direct sterilization, whether perpetual or temporary, whether of the man or of the woman." This included condoms, the Pill, sterilization, and any other unnatural form of obstructing conception.[9]

Sadly, there were people who left the Roman Catholic Church over *Humanae Vitae*, but this says far more about them than it does about the Church. If they were true Catholics, they would have accepted papal teaching, as challenging if ultimately fulfilling as this may have been. For many of them, the papal confirmation of the Catholic approach to sexuality contradicted their personal sex lives; they wanted the Church to accommodate them rather than to reform their own behaviour so as to accommodate the Church founded by Christ. Nobody said Christianity was easy. It's difficult to turn the other cheek, to forgive those who abuse you, to live a charitable and selfless life. All that was said was that sex was to be enjoyed in the context of love and with openness to God's plan. He gave us the ability to love and be sexually intimate, and we should repay him by using those gifts responsibly. This, it seems, was simply too much for some. It's very likely that those who left the Church over *Humanae Vitae,* and still leave over sexual issues, would not leave the Church over some statement of, for example, theology or foreign policy. How selfish and small, then, to abandon an institution that one is supposed to believe is God's instrument on earth just because it refuses to affirm someone's lust and because of a person's insistence on putting sexual convenience before consistent, moral, Christian precedent. Still, pride rather than principle has led thousands in the West to leave the Church. The Church, though, refuses to leave them.

Christian teaching against contraception was standard and not exclusively Catholic until the 1930s – the Anglicans softened their position at the 1930 Lambeth Conference due more to member activism than theological consideration and within seventy years became almost indifferent to Christian-based life teachings – but some evangelical denominations are now reconsidering their former approach to contraception. These Protestant churches have seen that apart from any Biblical arguments on the issue, the practical results are surprising but clear. Rather than liberating women – a frequent and leading argument made about the issue – contraceptives have tended to allow men to bring pressure to bear on women, telling girlfriends and partners that there is no chance of pregnancy so there is no reason why she shouldn't have sex with him if – yes, that old one – she really loved him. Rather than giving women more control over their sexuality, it's often allowed men to take even more power in the equation. The method of natural family planning advised by the Catholic Church is not the regularly mocked rhythm method – another outdated anti-Catholic cliché – but the Billings Ovulation Method in which women monitor their fertility, as well as their gynaecological health, and listen to the natural cycle and demands of their body. Unlike the Pill, it is entirely safe and gives control of a sexual relationship to the woman and not the man. It demands respect for women, for nature, and for the act itself, which by necessity becomes something other than habitual and commonplace.

There is, by the way, increasing medical evidence linking the contraceptive pill to women's medical problems, particularly in the area of breast cancer. It's bewildering how the Catholic Church that objects to the use of the Pill is accused of sexism while multinational drug companies who make a fortune out of a product that has millions of women putting alien chemicals into their bodies for decades, sometimes starting in the early teens, escape censure. The Pill fundamentally changes the way in which the female reproductive system is supposed to work and is often as much if not more for men's pleasure as for women's equality.[10]

Contrary to what critics might say, the Church does not demand large families and does not insist on what the more vulgar critics describe as "Catholic imperialism"; one theory is that Catholic teaching on contraception is part of some larger conspiracy to populate the world with Catholics. If you doubt that people believe this, take a look at any anti-Catholic website or just listen to general conversation. The truth is that contraception is in reality considered wrong because it violates natural law and contradicts the natural, God-given purpose of sex, which is procreation. The Church is the most human institution ever to exist, and it understands human nature because it was founded by He who created the world. Sex is fun, is supposed to be, and always will be. It's not just pornographers and prostitutes who appreciate the attraction of sex, and to abandon sexual pleasure to such people would be a moral disaster and a colossal surrender. The Church celebrates sexuality, celebrates fertility, and, most of all, celebrates the meeting of man and woman as one. It's baffling how we Catholics, who tend to have larger families than is the norm because of our open and fruitful attitudes to sex and love, are somehow supposed to be frightened and intimidated by sex while the aggressively childless or 1.2-kids brigade are allegedly the sexual experts. Put

bluntly, Catholics love it, revel in it, rejoice in its fecundity, positively dance in the joy and sweetness that is God's gift of sexual
intimacy within a love- and romance-filled marriage. Catholics
are not scared of sex but their neurotic, sexually confused opponents seem to be scared of Catholics.

Contraception is not new and was practised by cultures
as early as the ancient Egyptians and the Romans. Poisons,
sponges, condoms made of animal skins, and other such sexy
and appealing devices were used in an effort to prevent the creation of human life. The Bible opposed such activities from as
early as the Old Testament – the story of Onan and scripture's
condemnation of masturbation or coitus interruptus – and the
New Testament, and the early Church continued this position.
It's sometimes said that if an activity or belief is not specifically prohibited in the Bible then it cannot be wrong, which is
a breathtakingly absurd conclusion. The New Testament does
not have anything to say on all sorts of immoral behaviour,
partly because its writers did not have the space or the time,
partly because these issues are not directly pertinent but also
because some acts were so generally and obviously disapproved
of that to repeat the condemnation would have been redundant
if not insulting. Very few parents tell their children not to jump
off tall buildings, and it's terribly unusual to read a television
instruction manual that warns against hitting a friend over the
head with a television set. It doesn't mean that mums and dads
are fond of falling children or electronic companies advocate
murder in their name.

The Church fathers were certainly specific about the issue
of contraception. In AD 195, Clement of Alexandria wrote:
"Because of its divine institution for the propagation of man,
the seed is not to be vainly ejaculated, nor is it to be damaged,

nor is it to be wasted," and Hippolytus of Rome wrote in 255 on the subject of heresies and great errors: "On account of their prominent ancestry and great property, the so-called faithful want no children from slaves or lowborn commoners, they use drugs of sterility or bind themselves tightly in order to expel a fetus which has already been engendered." In AD 419 Augustine was absolute in his condemnation, and this from a man who had known the temptations of the world: "I am supposing, then, although you are not lying for the sake of procreating offspring, you are not for the sake of lust obstructing their procreation by an evil prayer or an evil deed. Those who do this, although they are called husband and wife, are not; nor do they retain any reality of marriage, but with a respectable name cover a shame. Sometimes this lustful cruelty, or cruel lust, comes to this, that they even procure poisons of sterility."

It's hardly a surprise that subjects such as contraception and abortion lead to such anger and frustration because they are directly personal and involve the most intimate and immediate forms of gratification and pleasure. Foreign wars, racist oppression, and mass injustice do affect us and should affect us more, but we are able to construct a distance, a fence of separation, between us and external issues that we find difficult to build when it's personal and concerns our daily life and our daily pleasure. But before anybody makes some grand, sweeping gesture about Catholics and abortion, Catholics and contraception, and Catholics and sex they should ask who it is – the Church or the modern, materialistic, and decadent world – that has confused its priorities. The sexual fanatics are those who obsess about sex and believe it to be morally neutral and have no inherent value. The Church believes that sex is so wonderful that it contains values as well as virtues.

We see this confusion of priorities at its most deadly at what is, as it were, the other end of the debate: euthanasia, mercy killing, compassionate homicide, assisted suicide. Pride hides beneath most that is wrong, from the thinnest of failings to the fattest of crime. Pride leads us to believe that we, rather than God, are always in control and that our bodies are ours to do with what we want, whenever we want. Sometimes this attitude is invincibly malicious, sometimes almost understandable. When it comes to the subject of euthanasia, we see both aspects. For those promoting what amounts to a cult of death, it is horror, pure and simple. For those who are suffering, the subject is far more complex and delicate. The arguments for euthanasia are perhaps better known than those against it because we hear them publicly articulated on a fairly regular basis. Implicit but perhaps not consciously so in this approach is the notion that disability is a curse, that we have the right and wisdom to make our own decisions about when to die, and that so-called mercy killing is administered only after layers of consideration. If at all possible, nobody approaching death should experience pain, and experts in the field now know that nobody need do so. All physical pain can be controlled but insufficient time and money is spent training doctors and nurses how to deal with end-of-life challenges.[11]

The proposition that a person who feels that they want to die is making an objective, informed decision about whether to live or die is fatuous. In reality, they are the least qualified people because they are, yes, so terrified and agonized that they want to die. Any of us who has experienced any sort of pain or nausea know that it is difficult to see beyond the immediate need to be free of distress. Beyond the physical pressures are the emotional ones – the feeling that one doesn't fit in any longer, the attitude that "I've had a good life, the children could do so much with the inheritance I'll leave behind, it costs them so much money to keep me in the home, and I know the grandchildren don't like coming all this way to visit me all the time." The media tells them that only the young and sexy matter, they are made to feel by television and radio that life is over by the age of seventeen, there are anti-aging stores opening on the main street, and then we wonder why elderly people feel rejected. A culture that once revered the aged as temples of wisdom now looks on them as slums of irrelevance. The answer is not to help someone die but help them to live.

It is no accident that the people most intimidated by, and active against, euthanasia are the disabled. While we boast equality, we violently discriminate against disability at the earliest opportunity by aborting babies that are considered imperfect and then attempt to pass legislation and create a cultural shift that would make the life of disabled people easier to terminate in their more mature years. In 1993, for example, Robert Latimer, a farmer in western Canada, killed his little girl Tracy. She had cerebral palsy but did not ask to die, was surrounded by people who loved her and even by extraordinary people who were willing to adopt her if her care became too difficult for the Latimers. Mr. Latimer put her in his truck, poisoned her to death with carbon monoxide, and then put her body into his wife's bed, hoping the girl's mother and the authorities would believe that Tracy had died naturally. His crime was discovered, and his defence was that he was putting her out of her misery when, of course, he was putting her out of his. When Latimer was arrested and charged and especially after he was imprisoned, media campaigns and petitions sprang up to support him. Almost all the time the defence was at work, it hardly ever mentioned the rights of the little girl who had been murdered. It took a child-writing in the *Vancouver Sun* newspaper in 1994 to show another side of the issue.

My name is Teague. I am 11 years old and have really severe cerebral palsy. The Latimer case in Saskatchewan has caused me a great deal of unhappiness and worry over the past few weeks. I feel very strongly that all children are valuable and deserve to live full and complete lives. No one should make the decision of another person about whether their life is worth living or not.

I have a friend who had CP and he decided that life was too hard and too painful. So he really let himself die. I knew he was leaving this world and letting himself dwell in the spiritual world. I told him that I understood that the spiritual world was really compelling, but that life was worth fighting for. I had to fight to live when I was very sick. The doctors said I wouldn't live long, but I knew I had so much to accomplish still.

I have to fight pain all the time. When I was little life was pain, I couldn't remember no pain. My foster Mom Cara helped me learn to manage and control my pain. Now my life is so full of joy. There isn't time enough in the day for me to learn and experience all I wish to. I have a family and many friends who love me. I have a world of knowledge to discover. I have so much to give.

I can't walk or talk or feed myself. But I am not "suffering from cerebral palsy." I use a wheel chair, but I am not "confined to a wheelchair." I have pain, but I do not need to be "put out of my misery."

My body is not my enemy. It is that which allows me

to enjoy Mozart, experience Shakespeare, savour a bouil-
labaisse feast and cuddle my Mom. Life is a precious gift.
It belongs to the person to whom it was given. Not to her
parents, nor to the state. Tracy's life was hers "to make of
it what she could." My life is going to be astounding.

We have to be extremely careful when we use terms like
quality of life because they are entirely subjective and, anyway,
largely without meaning. I see people who are physically and
mentally able all the time who have no obvious quality of life.
They seem to do no good to or for others, they are selfish, lazy,
foolish, rude, arrogant. Such a life does not seem to be one of
any genuine quality. Equally there are millions of people, often
living in slum conditions and working in mundane, empty jobs
whose quality of life may be questioned. Or wealthy, privileged
but spiritually bankrupt, vacuous men and women who contribute little but take so much. They appear to have no quality
of life and thus have no need to be alive. It depends who has the
power and who is able to make the decisions. In the 1890s and
early twentieth century, social engineers and eugenicists advocated an entire systematic program to eliminate those whom
they considered to be lacking in quality of life. The anti-Catholic
zealot and internationally renowned novelist H.G. Wells wrote
of the elimination not only of the mentally and physically ill
but of the sexually perverse, the black, brown and yellow, and
anybody who did not "fit in" with the new world of which he
dreamed. He was joined in these ambitions by Margaret Sanger,
the founder of Planned Parenthood and darling then and now
of feminism and abortion rights.[12]

Beyond the intellectually flimsy and morally dangerous
definition of *quality of life,* there are also semantic difficulties

with words such as *terminal*. One of the champions of euthanasia, Jack Kevorkian, when speaking to the National Press Club in Washington DC in 1992, said that a terminal illness was "any disease that curtails life even for a day," and the Hemlock Society, one of the largest and most active pro-euthanasia organizations in the world, frequently uses the word *terminal* as part of the phrase *terminal old age*, which has sweeping implications. Doctors generally admit that estimates of life expectancy are extremely difficult and dangerous to make, and although informed estimates of life expectancy certainly have a place in medicine, numerous people every year live far longer, even years longer, than expected. Sometimes this means a great deal more money is required to keep them alive and well, and that means more personal investment from families and more public investment from governments providing institutionalized health care and from insurance companies providing private insurance. The idea that financial concerns are not taken into account in the realm of euthanasia is naïve in the extreme. Then, of course, we have the slippery slope argument, often dismissed by supporters of euthanasia as being hysterical. Yet some slopes are slippery, very slippery indeed.

Margaret Somerville is a bioethicist of international reputation. In 2010, she wrote,

Although the need for euthanasia to relieve pain and suffering is the justification given, and the one the public accepts in supporting its legalization, research shows that dying people request euthanasia far more frequently because of fear of social isolation and of being a burden on others, than pain. So, should avoiding loneliness or being a burden count as a sufficient justification? Recently, some pro-euthanasia advocates have gone further, arguing that respect for people's rights to autonomy and self-determination means competent adults have a right to die at a time of their choosing, and the state has no right to prevent them from doing so. In other words, if euthanasia were legalized, the state has no right to require a justification for its use by competent, freely consenting adults.

For example, they believe an elderly couple, where the husband is seriously ill and the wife healthy, should be allowed to carry out their suicide pact. As Ruth von Fuchs, head of the Right to Die Society of Canada, stated, "Life is not an obligation." But although Ms. von Fuchs thought the wife should have an unfettered right to assisted suicide, she argued that it would allow her to avoid the suffering, grief, and loneliness associated with losing her husband – that is, she articulated a justification. We can see this same trend toward not requiring a justification – or, at least, nothing more than that's what a competent person over a certain age wants to do – in the Netherlands. Last month, a group of older Dutch academics and politicians launched a petition in support of assisted suicide for the over-70s who "consider their lives complete" and want to die. They quickly attracted more than 100,000 signatures, far more than needed to get the issue debated in the Dutch parliament. The Netherlands' 30-year experience with euthanasia shows clearly the rapid expansion, in practice, of what is seen as an acceptable justification for euthanasia.

[Somerville concluded,] Initially, euthanasia was limited to terminally ill, competent adults, with unrelievable pain and suffering, who repeatedly asked for euthanasia and gave their informed consent to it. Now, none of those requirements necessarily applies, in some cases not even in theory and, in others, not in practice. For instance, parents of severely disabled babies can request euthanasia for them, 12- to 16-year-olds can obtain euthanasia with parental consent, and those over 16 can give their own consent. More than 500 deaths a year, where the adult was incompetent or consent not obtained, result from euthanasia. And late middle-aged men (a group at increased risk for suicide) may be using it as a substitute for suicide. Indeed, one of the people responsible for shepherding through the legislation legalizing euthanasia in the Netherlands recently admitted publicly that doing so had been a serious mistake, because, he said, once legalized, euthanasia cannot be controlled. In other words, justifications for it expand greatly, even to the extent that simply a personal preference "to be dead" will suffice.

Life is not a sentence but a blessing. Death is guaranteed but to encourage it is a curse, especially for those who are most vulnerable and do not have access to power, money, friends, and even the basic tools of appeal. These are the most likely victims of euthanasia, those who are so ill as to have lost the ability to speak, write, and communicate. Father Frank Pavone from Priests for Life sums up their situation and how they should be treated by a civilized society very well. "What about them? That, indeed, is the question for the pro-euthanasia forces. People who cannot communicate are people. This gets to the heart of the problem. A person's inability to function does not make his life less valuable. People do not become 'vegetables.' Children of God never lose the divine image in which they were made."

Children of God: the Catholic attitude toward all of us, at every stage of life. When Pope John Paul II was approaching death, his once-fit, muscular body was bent, broken, and decaying. He had been a robust man who hiked, skied, and played soccer. He had resisted Nazis as well as Communists, helped bring down a Marxist regime that had murdered and incarcerated tens of millions, rejuvenated an entire Church, written books that changed the world, and visited country after country and continent after continent to spread the word of Catholicism. He had been shot, had suffered terrible health problems, and now felt the approach of death. Yet in all of his last year, in all of his last moments, he showed the great dignity that is there for all of us as we approach the end of this life's existence. He did not want to die but he was entirely content with death, because for the Catholic death is merely the beginning of the next stage of life. Beauty rather than euthanasia; grace rather than assisted suicide; joy rather than mercy killing.

If euthanasia receives a great deal of coverage in the media and the entertainment industry, the subject of homosexuality and the treatment of gay men and women takes up a degree of space that is staggering for a community that according to most credible estimates represents less than 3 per cent of the population. But compassion is especially necessary here for a whole variety of reasons, the most prominent one being that gay people deserve respect as men and women made in the image of God. Gay people live, love, feel, know sorrow and fear as well as happiness and triumph, contribute to society, and, like most people, generally try to be the best people they can be. There are all sorts of secular arguments used by the Catholic Church to respond to the issue of homosexuality, such as those the Church has outlined in resisting the demand so common in Europe, North and Latin America, and Australasia for same-sex marriage. Actually this challenge is not so much about the rights of a sexual minority but the status and meaning of marriage itself. Indeed, the deconstruction of marriage began not with the gay community asking for the right to marry but with the heterosexual world rejecting it. The term *common-law marriage* said it all. Marriage is many things but it is never common. Yet with this semantic and legal revolution, desire and convenience replaced commitment and dedication. The qualifications, so to speak, were lowered.

And one does have to qualify for marriage, just as one has, for example, to qualify for a pension or a military medal. People who have not reached the age of retirement don't qualify for a pension, people who don't serve in the armed forces don't qualify for a military medal. It's not a question of equality but requirement. A human right is intrinsic, a social institution is not. The four great and historic qualifications for marriage have always been number, gender, age, and blood: two people, male and female, over a certain age, and not closely related. Mainstream and responsible societies have sometimes changed the age of maturity, but incest has always been condemned and, by its nature, died out because of retardation. As for polygamy, it's making something of a comeback partly because of gay marriage and the subsequent expansion or loosening of what marriage is. Whenever this is mentioned by Catholics, we are accused of being extreme, but there is nothing extreme about it. Polygamy is an ancient tradition within Islam and was practised in Sephardic Judaism and some Asian cultures. When advocates of polygamy combine the precedent of gay marriage with the argument that true religious freedom includes the right of Muslim men to have more than one wife, it will be difficult, at least in the long term, to oppose it.

At the moment the international diaspora Muslim community is not sufficiently politically comfortable to pursue the issue, and the clearly deranged polygamous sects on the aesthetic as well as geographical fringes of society obscure any reasonable debate. But the argument will certainly come and the result is largely inevitable. If love is the only criterion for marriage, who are we to judge the love between one man and his wives? The state, though, in fact has a duty to judge and to do so based on its own interests, the most significant of which is its continued existence, meaning that we have to produce children. As procreation is the likely if not essential result of marriage between a man and a woman, it is in the interests of the state to encourage marriage.

Of course, gay couples can have an obliging friend assist them in having a baby, and gay men can adopt or have some other obliging friend have one for them, but this is hardly the norm and hardly going to guarantee the longevity of a stable society. Just as significantly, it smashes the fundamental concept of a child being produced through an act of love. The donation of bodily fluid by an anonymous person, or by that obliging friend again, is an act not of love but of lust, of indifference, or of profit. For the first time in world history, many countries are purposefully creating and legitimizing families where there will be either no male or no female role model and parent. Anyone who speaks of uncles, aunts, communities, and villages raising children has no real understanding of family life. Single-parent families exist and are sometimes excellent and it's also obviously the case that not every mother–father family is a success. But to consciously create unbalanced families where children can never enjoy the profound difference between man and woman, mother and father, is dangerous social engineering.

The Church teaches that homosexual desire is not sinful in itself, and that all sorts of people are tempted by sin and toward sinful lifestyles, and many of them are not sexual at all. It is the giving in to the temptation that creates the sin and blocks our relationship with God. The Old Testament refers to the sin of Sodom, where God was angry at the acts of homosexual intercourse that occurred in the city and eventually destroyed it. The episode is about more than homosexuality, for the Sodomites were also cruel and corrupt, but homosexuality was the major cause of God's displeasure. There are liberal theologians or, more strictly speaking, gay activists who make theological statements who will argue that the example of Sodom is more about lack of charity than it is about homosexuality, but this is wishful thinking on their part. It's significant that throughout Christian history, the only time this theory was proposed was when the gay rights movement became active. Hardly a coincidence. Leviticus also tells us, "You shall not lie with a male as with a woman; it is an abomination" and "If a man lies with a male as with a woman, both of them have committed an abomination; they shall be put to death, their blood is upon them." Perhaps so, respond critics, but the Old Testament also contains prohibitions on various foods, on mixing of clothing material, and even calls for attacks on rival tribes and peoples that are absurd or repugnant to modern ears. This is a sorry and sad understanding of history and of the Bible. The Old Testament is part history, part warning, and part tuition and is fulfilled by Christ in the New Testament. Everything we see in the Old should be understood through the prism of the New – interpretation through the other end of the telescope as it were. All sorts of cosmetic, ceremonial, and era-related aspects of the book do not apply any more, but the moral code taught in the Old Testament is vital and timeless. By the logic of the revisionists we need not observe all the Ten Commandments; mind you, that seems to be the attitude of some of these same liberal theologians today.

The New Testament is just as specific about homosexuality; Paul in his letter to the Romans writes, "For this reason God gave them up to dishonourable passions. Their women exchanged natural relations for unnatural, and the men likewise gave up natural relations with women and were consumed with passion for one another, men committing shameless acts with men and receiving in their own persons the due penalty for their error. And since they did not see fit to acknowledge God, God gave them up to a base mind and to improper conduct" and "Though they know God's decree that those who do such things deserve to die, they not only do them but approve those who practise them." He is forgiving and understanding of all sorts of failings but reminds people again when discussing homosexuality, "Do you not know that the wicked will not inherit the kingdom of God? Do not be deceived: Neither the sexually immoral nor idolaters nor adulterers nor male prostitutes nor homosexual offenders nor thieves nor the greedy nor drunkards nor slanderers nor swindlers will inherit the kingdom of God." The response from some in the gay community is that the translations are not always accurate and that Paul and his contemporaries lived at a time when we did not understand homosexuality or sexuality in general and that the modern Christian world should adapt to a post-sexual revolutionary world. Again, there is a fundamental problem of logic here. The translations are precisely accurate, and Paul was not referring to male prostitution or to the sexual abuse of young men but to homosexuality.

As for Paul and the other early Christians not understanding homosexuality with the benefit of modern sophistication, does this also apply to his understanding of love, forgiveness, sacrifice, helping the poor and the marginalized, embracing our enemies, rejecting greed, searching for truth and goodness, and believing that Jesus Christ was the Messiah? He said and wrote about all these things but if he was wrong and so irrelevant and confined to his time when discussing homosexuality, why would any of his other opinions hold any credence today? God put His Son and His Son's apostles and disciples on earth at a particular time and for a particular reason. Anachronism is the enemy and not the friend of liberal scholars.

Apart from the negative references to homosexuality in scripture and the overwhelming number of condemnations of it in Church history throughout most of the two thousand years of Christendom, there are also calls for the alternative: for sexual union between men and women, for procreation, for family, and for a human manifestation of the creation story. As has been mentioned before, the Catholic Church believes in and teaches natural law and that humans were made, naturally, to complement each other as men and women. Our physical differences and sexual and biological capabilities are not mere accidents but God-given gifts. They are to be relished and enjoyed but not abused and twisted. It is not homophobic to courteously and gently explain the Catholic objection to same-sex relationships any more than it is a form of phobia to speak out against other behaviour considered sinful by Christianity. This is painful for many gay people to hear, which is why the discussion must be handled with empathy and compassion. Yet the word *homophobia* is thrown around carelessly, often not to describe a bigoted and violent person who hates gay men and women but to silence anybody who has an objection to some aspect of the gay lifestyle. Thus it is a form of censorship and makes the Catholic, not the gay person, the victim in all this. Throughout Europe and North America, there have been attempts, often successful, to close down Catholic and other Christian organizations that may perform outstanding charitable work – Catholic social services, the Salvation Army, and so on – but who refuse to affirm same-sex marriage or give children as adoptees to gay couples. Priests, bishops, and ordinary Catholic laypeople have been taken to human rights commissions, fired, or even arrested and charged for speaking out on issues of homosexuality.

This is without a doubt not the desire of all gay people, and many are revolted by the heavy hand of political correctness. But they have also suffered over the years, and however delicate and empathetic the explanation of Catholic teaching may be, the words will sound harsh and perhaps be of limited comfort to a gay person. Many but not all gay people believe that they were born homosexual and that God does not make mistakes. He doesn't. Actually, we have no idea whether people are born homosexual or not, and because the study of homosexuality is so politically controlled now, we probably never will – to suggest it is a mental illness or can be cured, for example, has led to and would probably still lead to dismissal from most registered psychiatric associations. Some people do seem to have same-sex attractions from an extremely early age, others admit to embracing the lifestyle and the preference much later. Whatever the case, it is essential that respect and understanding are always used in this discussion.

Sexuality and sexual desire are part of all of us, just as is original sin. We are a broken people in a fallen world, but because the Roman Catholic Church admits this, it is not always popular. The catechism states, "Basing itself on sacred scripture, which presents homosexual acts as acts of grave depravity, tradition has always declared that homosexual acts are intrinsically disordered. They are contrary to the natural law. They close the sexual act to the gift of life. They do not proceed from a genuine affective and sexual complementarity. Under no circumstances can they be approved." It goes on to acknowledge that the homosexual "psychological genesis remains largely unexplained" and that "the number of men and women who have deep-seated homosexual tendencies is not negligible. This inclination, which is objectively disordered, constitutes for most of them a trial. They must be accepted with respect, compassion, and sensitivity. Every sign of unjust discrimination in their regard should be avoided. These persons are called to fulfill God's will in their lives and, if they are Christians, to unite to the sacrifice of the Lord's cross the difficulties that they may encounter from their condition. Homosexual persons are called to chastity. By the virtues of self-mastery that teach them inner freedom, at times by the support of disinterested friendship, by prayer and sacramental grace, they can and should gradually and resolutely approach Christian perfection." These are hard but true words about a story with an ending yet to be written.

CATHOLICS AND OTHER STUFF

AND WHAT OTHER STUFF there is. Why is the Church so wealthy, wasn't there a woman Pope, what is an annulment, what on earth are indulgences and does that mean you can buy them and buy your way into heaven? Is the *Da Vinci Code* true, are Catholics concerned about the rights of animals, why do we suffer, and did Jesus even exist in the first place? And on and on and on. There isn't room to repeat, let alone answer, every question, but I can address some of the more common ones.

It's appropriate to begin with a few basic facts about Jesus Christ and whether He existed or not. Almost every discovery in the last hundred and fifty years in the field of Biblical archaeology appears to prove the Bible right, even to the point of surprising serious and orthodox Christian and Jewish scholars. It's been oddly pathetic observing liberal panic as another dig in the Middle East puts flesh to the bones of scripture. As for Jesus Himself, there are some absolute truths here. Jewish records refer to Jesus of Nazareth and did so even before Christ's own followers had written about Him. Obviously these Jewish sages did not believe that Jesus was the Messiah, but they refer to him quite clearly as the son of Mary, the alleged father being a man we know little about. Then we have Josephus, a Jewish general who betrayed his people and became a friend of the

Romans and, indeed, a Roman himself. His writings are vital for any understanding of the Jews in the first century but must be placed in context. Josephus mentions Jesus, the Jesus, in his writings. It is almost certain that later writers, Christian enthusiasts, revised his words to make them seem more pro-Christian. Hence in some obviously edited versions of his work, Josephus, a Jewish man, suddenly sounds like a Christian. He was not, and these expansions of his references to Jesus are to be dismissed.[1]

The point, however, is that it is the revisions and not the original statements that should be expunged from the debate. Josephus knew of Jesus because no observer of the time could not know of Him. He refers to Jesus' ministry and to Jesus' followers. Some people have tried to throw out the baby with the bathwater, resulting in their entire argument becoming rather wet. Next is the Roman historian Tacitus. He discusses the great fire in Rome, how Nero was thought responsible and how the emperor blamed the Christians, named after Christus, who was crucified by "one of our governors, Pontius Pilate." The Roman biographer Seutonius also refers to Jesus and a riot across the Tiber by supporters and foes of Christianity. Pliny the younger, governor of Asia Minor, also speaks of Christ and Christians. Then there is the Gospel evidence for Jesus. The Gospels were written by supporters, of course, but the more we learn about them the earlier we can place them and the more authentic they are shown to be. New research and the latest discoveries tell us so very much. The remarkable Ryland Papyrus on the Nile includes parts of John's Gospel. Serious scholars now agree that the Gospels were completed well before AD 100 – that is, while some who were present during Christ's life still lived. Further, these were produced for communities composed of people who knew Jesus or whose parents told them stories of personal witness and intimate experience of Jesus.[2]

In fact no Biblical expert – nor historian – worth the name doubts that Jesus lived, that He claimed to be the Messiah, and that many who knew Him believed that claim. The idea that He was just a great moral teacher or that we can believe some but not all of what He taught is based not on consistent thought but on a desire to be a comfortable follower of a figure whose life and death has little do with our "comfort." Think of the distressing impact of Jesus' claim to be the Son of God. If He wasn't, He was lying or insane. Liars are not to be believed and madmen are not to be followed even in part. But should we believe? Consider the first-generation martyrs. People die for the wrong reasons, but they assume them to be the right reasons. If their faith in any idea or any person can be broken, they are no longer willing to make the ultimate sacrifice. Yet men and women who knew Jesus, lived with Him, saw Him die and rise again were willing to go to their deaths with a smile. This is important. The followers of Christ were in chaos when they saw their master crucified like a common criminal. It was the resurrection, an event He had promised, that thrust them into belief and, frequently, a martyr's death. There is no explanation for the documented martyrdom of those who knew Jesus other than that they believed, without doubt, that He was the Messiah and that He had been raised from the dead because they were there. They were not few in number and they were not slow of wit. They were intelligent, street-wise people: dockworkers, fisherman, former terrorists and prostitutes, collaborating bureaucrats and brilliant teachers. They knew. They knew the sight and smell of death, knew when people were dead, and saw their friend and the man they loved dead. Then they saw Him alive again.

They knew He was God because He's called that seven times in the New Testament and is referred to as being divine on dozens of occasions. He was crucified not for being a prophet or an ethicist, or for that matter a champion of social justice, but for claiming to be the Son of God. Numerous letters from pagan and presumably objective or even hostile writers from the first and second centuries, including one written to the Emperor Marcus Aurelius, who died in AD 180, describe how Christians believe Jesus to be divine. And no, contrary to what Dan Brown's risible novel *The Da Vinci Code* might tell us, the Gnostic Gospels did not frequently mention that Jesus was married to Mary Magdalene. In fact, those Gnostic Gospels, so often quoted in movies and by conspiracy theorists, were rejected by the Church for a variety of reasons, primarily because they were distorted reworkings of the four Gospels and not the least because they were often misogynistic, were frequently contradictory, and tended to be self-serving and excruciatingly dull.[3]

Anti-Catholics also tell us that the Emperor Constantine collated the Bible and pretty much got the Church started. This would be news to the Emperor Constantine. The Old Testament, of course, existed even before the birth of Jesus, and the collection of texts into the New Testament began at the end of the first century – with most of the books agreed on within the next fifty years. The compilation was not finalized until the end of the fourth century. Constantine, however, died in AD 337. In other words, there is no way that he could have compiled the Bible even if he wanted to or had the ability to do so. What he certainly did do was to commission Bishop Eusebius to make fifty copies of the Bible that already existed so that more people could read it.

Speaking of Dan Brown and *The Da Vinci Code* – and speaking briefly because even though he's influenced so many people he doesn't really deserve the attention – his claim in his book that "the royal bloodline of Jesus Christ has been chronicled in exhaustive detail by scores of historians" is just silly. The historians he lists in his book are Margaret Starbird, Richard Leigh, Henry Lincoln, Clive Prince, Lynn Picknett, and Michael Baigent. The problem is that just like Dan Brown, these aren't really historians. Baigent has a basic degree in psychology and is working on an MA in mysticism, and Picknett and Prince are best known for their work on the occult and UFOs. Pretending to be a scholar of Hebrew, Brown also writes that YHWH, the Jewish sacred name for God, is based on the word Jehovah. And Jehovah, he says, is a combination of the masculine Jah and the feminine Havah, signifying Eve. Thus God gave us feminism, Jesus was a pioneer of progressive gender politics, and the Roman Catholic Church has hidden all this to preserve male power and exclude women, particularly Mary Magdalene, from their rightful place in society and culture. Fun for the credulous but not at all true. YHWH doesn't come from Jehovah but Jehovah from YHWH. The word was used thousands of years before *Jehovah* came into existence, which was as late as the sixteenth century. Dan Brown also writes that the Priory of Sion was founded in early medieval Europe. Untrue again. It was registered with the French government in a dusty office in 1956. His central bad guy is an Opus Dei monk. Hardly. Opus Dei is an overwhelmingly lay organization and they have no monks. Let me repeat, there is no such thing as an Opus Dei monk. Brown states that five million women were killed by the Church as witches. In fact, modern research has shown that the witch hunts began in the sixteenth century in Europe and that between 30,000 and 50,000 men and women were burned to death for the crime of witchcraft. However, 90 per cent of those trials took place before secular tribunals in countries such as Germany and France where by the 1500s the Church had lost most of its influence in judicial matters. Indeed, it was precisely in countries like Spain and Italy where the Catholic Church still had influence that there were almost no witchcraft trials. He refers to the Pope in the Vatican long before the Pope lived in the Vatican. And the list goes on.[4]

On Opus Dei, Dan Brown is particularly awful, but then Opus Dei seems to be a favourite target for Catholic-bashers in general. If it didn't exist, they'd have to invent it and then invent a movie about it. Literally "Work of God," the institution was founded by a Spanish priest named Josemaría Escrivá in 1928 as a largely lay organization of Roman Catholics with the purpose of seeking holiness in one's ordinary work and maintaining orthodoxy within their faith. Holiness is within the grasp of everyday people, doing everyday things, said the founder, but they need guidance. It is now an international prelature with houses and followers throughout the world. It has roughly 86,000 members, around 1,800 of them priests. It is a personal prelature that depends directly on the Vatican, which means that it has official backing from the highest quarters. To understand Opus Dei, one has to understand that Catholicism is not always the theologically homogenous organization some make it out to be. Certainly for the last hundred years, there has been a division between liberal and conservative, something of which Escrivá was keenly aware. His followers claim that Opus Dei is very much within the spirit of Vatican II, the Church council that, it was said, opened up the windows of the Church and let in the light of change. Opus Dei places enormous significance on the sacraments, the rosary, and strict moral discipline, which is unsettling for the secular world perhaps but at the heart, and of course the soul, of the Roman Catholic Church.

This kind of faithfulness is also uncomfortable for those liberals who find themselves increasingly detached from vibrant and living Catholicism. It's ironic, but the so-called progressives are now seen as old-fashioned and out of date, preaching a religious relativism that has little relevance, particularly to the young. Opus Dei, on the other hand, establishes schools and programs in inner cities, performs charity work in the developing world, and certainly does a great deal of good. It and other orthodox groups are growing almost as fast as liberal Catholicism is declining.[5] Critics, though, argue that it is cult-like. This isn't fair.

Actual membership certainly is demanding and is only for those who are committed to taking their faith seriously. Some members (a small percentage of the total) commit themselves to celibacy and devote a certain part of their income to Opus Dei but doing so is entirely voluntary. There have been cases of vulnerable people embracing the movement and perhaps hurting their families, but this is not really the fault of Opus Dei. There have also been rumours of fascist sympathies within the organization. Again, just not true. Because of the Spanish origins of Opus Dei, it is strong in Latin America and, of course, in Spain itself. General Franco did use Opus Dei members in his cabinet, but long after he had largely abandoned the far right and was seeking to modernize his country. Opus Dei members have also faced deportation and worse because of their stand for social justice in Latin American dictatorships.[6] But back to more sensible matters than Mr. Brown's fantasies about albino monks and cultish Catholics.

The problem of suffering. The terrible problem of awful, painful, seemingly pointless suffering. Bad things often happen to good people and just as often good things happen to bad people. A true Catholic response would be to acknowledge that this circumstance is difficult and challenging but also to ask why it should be anything of a surprise. The Bible makes it quite clear that faith in Jesus Christ and in His Church does not guarantee a good life but a perfect eternity. In fact, there is more prediction in scripture of struggle on earth for the believer than there is of gain and success. There are Christian sects that promise material wealth and all sorts of triumph in exchange for faith, but this has never been something that Catholicism would affirm. Roman Catholics believe that this life on earth is only the land of shadows and that real life hasn't begun yet. Suffering in this sinful world is surely more of a problem for the atheist, or the anti-Catholic, who thinks that this life is all that there is and all that matters and that at death we are mere dust, food for worms, nothing. This idea of an afterlife could, of course, just be a crutch on which Catholics lean so as to give their lives and their suffering some meaning. It's an accusation frequently tossed at Catholics and Christians in general. But lack of faith could just as well be a crutch for non-believers, allowing them to live their lives without any concept of accountability and giving them some sort of false confidence. The difference is that while Catholicism has an abundance of intellectual underpinnings to support its arguments, anti-Catholicism and atheism have few if any. The idea that people of faith have never before encountered suffering and that when the "why do bad things happen to good people" argument is made we will all suddenly look stunned and abandon our faith is ridiculous. The book of Job is full of such cries to God and questions about pain and suffering, and Christ Himself on the cross asks, "My God, my God, why have you abandoned me?" It is fully understandable to feel anguish at times of pain, but if we think further we surely have to ask whether suffering and death are the worst things in an existence that is eternal. Pain is an emotion, and emotions allow us all sorts of joy as well as lack of joy and the opposite of joy. Pain is also a warning sign and a way to protect us against danger. That something may hurt is undeniable, that we will all feel some sort of pain at some point is inevitable, but whether this pain is our doing or God's is something entirely different. Why, we are asked, would an all-knowing, all-powerful, all-good God allow us to suffer? Easy. He allows us all sorts of things because we have the freedom to behave as we will, but He has also provided a place with the greatest contentment we can imagine if only we listen to Him, to His Son, and to His Church.

We have free will because God is love, and no lover would allow anything else. A man who locks his wife in a room is not a lover but an abuser. God wants us to return to Him but cannot force us to take this course, and if we choose an eternity without Him we have chosen hell. When we do, we then abuse the God in whom we do not believe for allowing us to choose to spend our future away from Him in a place we have chosen ourselves. "God, God, God, you are so awful and why have you created hell? Oh, and by the way I don't believe in you." Our pride and our rejection of God are ours alone. As a loving father, He gives us the freedom to choose. I sometimes recall the first time my wife and I allowed our eldest son to go to school alone on public transport. He was old enough and we had to let him go. I was waiting at the front door by the middle of the afternoon. He came in at the appropriate time, ignored his father in the way boys of that age are supposed to, and then went up to his room. We had to let him go on his own, but our relief when he returned is hard to describe. Imagine, then, how God must feel when we come back to Him.

We are people, made in His image, to love Him and to be loved by Him. Which brings us to the modern fashion of animal rights and the accusation that the Catholic Church cares more about men and women than it does about animals. Of course it does, just as it should do. This isn't an accusation at all but a statement of rational and Catholic belief. The argument that care for animals and care for humans are part of some inevitable continuum simply isn't true but it's helped us to escalate our empathy for animals to a hysterical, pagan level at the direct expense of people. There is something fundamentally contrary to Christian virtue in all of this, because as creatures made in the image of God, we ought to feel a greater spark of love and understanding for our brothers and sisters than we do for animals. It has little to do with vulnerability because even the suffering of babies is frequently ignored or even justified by people who routinely weep for rabbits. If they are unborn babies, the comparison with cats doesn't even register. Christ died to free us from our sins, not to assuage our sentimentality. We see this echoed in international policy as well as in daily reaction. To ignore the suffering of an animal is inhuman, but to obsess about the suffering of an animal is anti-human. Yet this is what we do, even to the point of creating an entire ideology around the hideous misnomer of animal rights. The notion of rights is a human construct and human rights can apply, obviously, only to humans. Because we are distinct and superior, we have to act in a compassionate way toward animals, but this demands use rather than abuse, not a fantasy inclusion of animals into human society. Babies matter more than kittens, children of the poor matter more than pets of the rich, humans are more deserving of life and liberty than sharks and ants. By the way, it's deeply significant that cuddly critters induce more sympathy than ugly ones. Cuteness appears to be the measure of an animal's right to life. Or on a good day the criteria might be based on how intelligent they are – dolphins and dogs being kings of the cause. Yet if this is the measure, humans being the most intelligent of creatures must then deserve the most respect.

As the most important and most inalienable right is that to life, we cannot avoid the jarring difference between our over-reaction to what is usually a civilized treatment of animals and our indifference to the killing of the unborn. Simply, abortion mills are worse than puppy mills. To expose this neurotic, perverse juxtaposition, however, is to invite mockery and anger. "Not that old issue again, nobody cares about abortion." Then another radio phone-in show about how animals do less harm to the planet than men and women. We are a product of God's plan, as are animals. To reverse the order of His intentions and His creation is not only a denial of Him but another example of selfish, pampered, Western foolishness, Disney instead of decency. Christ fed the multitude; it was they who had rights and who were hungry, the fish didn't really matter that much. It's straightforward, it's humane, it's sensible, it's Catholic.

If the Catholic Church's apparent inability to grapple with animal liberation doesn't send us running out of the pews – and if it does, we didn't know why we were there in the first place – we're hit with the old regular that the Church is dripping with money while the rest of the world starves. The Church is committed to the needy and the poor, and the apparent wealth of the Catholic Church is not only irrelevant to this but also inaccurate. Most priests, nuns, monks, and others who work in the service of the Catholic Church do so for a very low wage. They often work extraordinarily long hours and spend their retirement years in modest care homes. There is obviously a great deal of wealth in Rome at the Vatican, open for everybody to see in the museums – most of which operate at a deficit – and exhibitions of paintings, sculptures, and beautiful works of art. Much of this work is the creation of Catholic artists who wanted their achievements to be in the Vatican and on display to the rest of the world. The Church has preserved this art for centuries as the patrimony of humanity; if it hadn't done so, much of it would have been destroyed, stolen, or bought by private collectors and never seen by the majority of people. It does not belong only to the Church today but to the Church of all time and for all time to come. To sell it for cash and have it hidden away for a selection of the elite seems a bizarre idea. These works of art simply aren't in the gift of the Catholic Church to sell. If they were and if they were sold, the money raised could be given to good causes but it would soon be spent and forgotten, whereas the art collections in the Vatican are there forever.

The Catholic Church is one of the most generous organizations in the world, giving an enormously high percentage of what it raises to charities. The collections raised every Sunday at Masses throughout the world go to maintaining often leaky churches but also to running soup kitchens and aid centres and to help and support the needy and desperate. The Catholic Church built and ran hospitals, schools, and centres for the poor and unemployed generations before the secular state became involved, and even today a visit to almost any main street in the Western world or to a village or town in the developing world will show Catholic charities and outreach organizations operating in what are often the most challenging of conditions. It is estimated, for example, that most of the help given to people with AIDS in Africa comes from Catholics and the Catholic Church. We also have to realize that while Jesus reached out to the poor, He was not some economic revolutionary whose role was to remove poverty and create an alternative economic structure. This is chauvinism and arrogance on our part – to believe that if Christ wanted to eliminate poverty He could have done so in a moment. He was a Messiah and not a Marxist. In the book of Matthew, when a woman approaches Jesus with a jar full of costly ointment to be poured on His head, there was anger from some of those around Him. This is a waste, they said, and the money could be spent on other, better, more worthwhile things such as helping the poor. "Why do you trouble the woman?" asks Jesus. "For she has done a beautiful thing to me. For you always have the poor with you, but you will not always have me."

The Catholic Church is well aware of the attempt to politicize Christ: Jesus the neo-conservative who is used by people to support their interests in the free market and Anglo-American superiority; Jesus the rebel whose name is exploited by those working tirelessly against climate change or for international socialism; Jesus the me, Jesus the mine, Jesus the mere tool to be used to oil the mechanism of my particular political obsession. For the fanatical Israel-basher, He is Christ the Palestinian militant, for the Christian Zionist He is Jesus the Israeli warrior. And so on and so on until we leave the real meaning of our Lord far, far behind. He was and is God. This is the whole point and explains why He was here. He told this to His followers time and time again and some of them just wouldn't listen!

Once we try to belittle him and to transform God into some political icon or cause figurehead, we are committing the most vile and vulgar of sins: pride and the absolute certainty that our passing beliefs are more significant than the life, death, and essential meaning of Christ Jesus.

Christ was crucified for one reason and one reason alone, and to misunderstand this is to misunderstand Christianity. His death was part of God's plan to give His Son to die for our sins so as to make us clean and to enable us to find salvation and our way back to our creator. He was crucified because He claimed to be the Messiah. The Romans would rather have let Him go. There were myriad political prisoners and activists in the region at the time, some of whom were outraged that the Son of God said that the poor would always be with us, that His kingdom was not of this earth, and that while social justice was important, spiritual completion was paramount. From the mid-1960s until perhaps ten or fifteen years ago, so-called liberal ideas dominated Roman Catholic thinking and enabled this confusion and misunderstanding to take hold. White, privileged people were telling the rest of the world what Christianity meant and simultaneously failing to see the irony of their arrogance. Just as the Church of England was once described as the Tory party at prayer, this was socialism liturgically dancing around the altar. It was very much the other side of the same coin that in the 1930s insisted that Catholicism meant support for General Franco, for anti-Semitism, and for perennial counter-revolution.

That nonsense was no more Catholic than are amateur theologians dressing their politics in the seamless cloak of Christ. By all means be left or right but do not try to use or abuse Jesus Christ by giving Him honorary political party status. The result of all this was the mass, and Mass, defection of good people who wanted the Gospel from the Catholic Church but instead received the manifesto. Those ideas are now passé, and the ideologues behind them – usually good and well-meaning people but so naïve and destructive – tend to be older and on the point of retirement. The damage done is being repaired but some of the exiles may never return. This was self-indulgence rather than true indulgence and a huge loss to the Church.

The word *indulgence,* of course, tends to conjure up images of brave Protestant reformers arguing that the evil Catholic Church is so greedy and so in need of money that it is willing to sell indulgences to people to ease them into heaven. As is so often the case, this is hardly an accurate picture of what happened. The Church defines an indulgence as "a remission before God of the temporal punishment due to sins whose guilt has already been forgiven, which the faithful Christian who is duly disposed gains under certain defined conditions through the Church's help when, as a minister of redemption, she dispenses and applies with authority the treasury of the satisfactions won by Christ and the saints." It's theological nonsense that someone can buy their way out of God's judgment and escape hell. An indulgence can be earned on Earth to compensate for the punishment due for sins that would otherwise need to be atoned for in purgatory, and they were conceived as a way of dealing with this exact issue, to replace some of the more severe penances that were common in the early Church.[7]

There had certainly been abuses of indulgences, and that is why the Council of Trent in 1567 brought forth reforms to make it clear that any indulgences that had been the result of money being exchanged were invalid. To gain an indulgence you must be a Catholic in a state of grace and have the full intention of performing the act for which the indulgence is given.

A partial indulgence must be carried out with what is known as "a contrite heart"; a plenary indulgence requires the same contrite heart but also requires the person receiving it to go to confession, receive Holy Communion, and pray for the Pope, usually with an Our Father and Hail Mary. The Catechism of the Church says this: "The Christian who seeks to purify himself of his sin and to become holy with the help of God's grace is not alone. 'The life of each of God's children is joined in Christ and through Christ in a wonderful way to the life of all the other Christian brethren in the supernatural unity of the Mystical Body of Christ, as in a single mystical person.'"

A far more distressing issue for people today is the perceived stand of the Church on divorce and annulment, a particularly pressing issue given the alarming rates of divorce in the Western world and the common desire to remarry. The latter, the desire to remarry, is usually where Catholic teaching is most misunderstood and unfairly criticized. Many people who regard themselves as being Catholic assume that the Catholic Church is there to marry them, baptize their children, and be nicely decorated for Christmas and Easter but they also presume that this same Church has no right to refuse their requests and wishes even if those requests and wishes directly contradict the teachings and requirements of the Roman Catholic Church. As has been said before, nobody is forced to be a Catholic, but if you want to be a Catholic you have to live as a Catholic. And the institution of marriage has particular significance in the life of Catholics because it is a sacrament of the Catholic Church. A sacrament, according to the catechism, is an "efficacious [sign] of grace, instituted by Christ and entrusted to the Church, by which divine life is dispensed to us. The visible rites by which the sacraments are celebrated signify and make present the graces proper to each sacrament. They bear fruit in those who receive them with the required dispositions." In other words, marriage is a holy encounter with Christ that makes people holy. Holiness is about God – and being about God is serious – indeed ultimately serious business. God is faithful – we are to be faithful. That is the stuff of holiness. Thus, of the sacrament of marriage Jesus said, "Every one who divorces his wife and marries another commits adultery, and he who marries a woman divorced from her husband commits adultery," and Paul stated, "Thus a married woman is bound by law to her husband as long as he live" and "Accordingly, she will be called an adulteress if she lives with another man while her husband is alive."

The early Church was equally strong in its language. Clement of Alexandria in AD 208: "That Scripture counsels marriage, however, and never allows any release from the union, is expressly contained in the law: 'You shall not divorce a wife, except for reason of immorality.' And it regards as adultery the marriage of a spouse, while the one from whom a separation was made is still alive. 'Whoever takes a divorced woman as wife commits adultery,' it says; for 'if anyone divorce his wife, he debauches her'; that is, he compels her to commit adultery. And not only does he that divorces her become the cause of this, but also he that takes the woman and gives her the opportunity of sinning; for if he did not take her, she would return to her husband." Clement is just continuing the teaching of Justin Martyr more than fifty years earlier: "In regard to chastity, [Jesus] has this to say: 'If anyone look with lust at a woman, he has already before God committed adultery in his heart.' And, 'Whoever marries a woman who has been divorced from another husband, commits adultery.' According to our Teacher, just as they are sinners who contract a second marriage, even though it be in accord with human law, so also are they sinners who look with lustful desire at a woman. He repudiates not only one who actually commits adultery, but even one who wishes to do so; for not only our actions are manifest to God, but even our thoughts."[8]

The Roman Catholic Church believes that marriage is for life. It is the coming together of two people as one flesh, the popular and intimate manifestation of God's plan for creation. It's not to be taken lightly, in spite of what modern fashions tell us and in spite of the pressures that are applied to today's marriages. Nor does it have anything to do with property rights, male dominance, or any other tendentious and misleading political and sociological propaganda that has been fed to us in recent years. Marriage as we know it today existed and was taught by the Church long before feminist theory became such fun. Thus the termination of a marriage matters a great deal, even if some of those experiencing the understandable pain of a separation wished otherwise. An annulment is the conclusion by a Church tribunal that what was assumed to be a valid marriage in the eyes of the Roman Catholic Church was not. Because marriage seems so disposable today, we find it hard to understand why the Church is so adamant about it, but this says far more about modern values than about the timeless, grace-filled view of marriage. Some marriages obviously cannot remain together – where, for example, abuse occurs. But we know that children suffer when marriages break up and that they are torn between two parents who are living apart and sometimes fighting for the love or custody of their children. The immediate and long-term psychological consequences of such experiences are becoming increasingly evident. The Church puts children at the centre of marriage and family but also puts great importance on marriage itself. It cannot, though, have any influence over whether someone gets divorced or not and, contrary to what some people think or try to convince others is true, this area really has nothing to do with Catholicism in the strictest sense – apart from the Church's concern for the state of society and the well-being of members of that society. It becomes a Catholic issue when people who are divorced want to remarry in the Catholic Church.

An annulment does not prove that the two people who were married did not love each other, it does not involve the Church choosing or taking sides, it does not lead the Church to hold one party guilty and one innocent, and the Church does not judge husband or wife as being better or worse Catholics. None of this is relevant. Annulment is the finding that when the marriage occurred, one or both of the people involved did not have the full capacity for a Catholic marriage, that they did not give their consent, or in some way did not fulfil the Church's requirements for a valid marriage. This is where a great deal of misunderstanding tends to arise. An annulment doesn't mean that a meaningful relationship never existed and certainly doesn't imply that if there are children from that relationship they are illegitimate. The following is extremely important. A divorce is a device of the secular state authority and ends something that existed and states that a marriage is over. An annulment is a statement by the Church that the marriage that has broken down in fact never existed as a sacramental reality in the first place. The reason may be that someone was pressured into marriage, was drunk or on drugs, was lied to, was too immature to make such a decision, may have married to escape a home atmosphere that was threatening or abusive, may have married under any sort of false pretence, that the marriage took place even though one of the partners had no intention of being faithful or was using their partner for financial gain or to earn a passport or citizenship, or if either husband or wife had no intention of having any children – an openness to children being a prerequisite for a valid Catholic marriage. An inability to have children, however, is not the same thing and in no way makes a marriage invalid. None of this presents the Church as being draconian or lacking in sensitivity but nor can or would the Church accept some excuses such as "We've grown apart," "I love someone else," or "The sex just isn't as good anymore." It can't because it's Catholic and Catholicism teaches that marriage is given to us by God and should not be taken lightly by His creatures.

No person has to apply for an annulment and not everyone who does will be granted one. There is a lot of mythology around the subject, usually based on the rumour that wealthy people can buy annulments and those with friends in high places in the Catholic Church can get them too easily. Other people, runs the argument, who lack money or powerful friends can wait decades and their lives can be ruined. Or, we're told, annulments are meaningless and are just a facade the Church uses to make it look as though it cares about marriage and divorce. Actually the system is efficient and fairly speedy, and those involved in the tribunals take their jobs very seriously. The process is non-adversarial and entails a great deal of compassionate counselling of people going through this oh-so-painful rupture. Because of this, the process can take a little time but this is, after all, a highly important decision. No matter how rich or important a Catholic may be, they have to go through the same hearing as the poorest and most anonymous fellow member of the Church. If the Catholic Church maintained the whole annulment approach only for the sake of appearance, it would be an elaborate and costly waste of time. Remember, any number of people tragically leave the Church every year because they are told that their marriage was valid and that, while they should but do not have to stay together, they cannot obtain a state divorce and then hope to be remarried in a Catholic Church. This tends to lead to Catholics becoming Anglican or other types of Protestant, where marriage is respected but is not truly sacramental.

This is all very sad, but the Church cannot become less Catholic for the sake of expediency. A divorced person who is not remarried can still receive the Catholic sacraments and even a Catholic who has been divorced and remarried without an annulment can still live a Catholic life, attend Mass, read scripture, and lead a moral life. They cannot, however, receive the sacraments – they come, as it were, as a package and we can't pick and choose which ones we'll observe and which ones we won't. If this sounds exclusive or elitist, it is, but the exclusivity comes from the individual and not the Church. The Roman Catholic Church allows people to exclude themselves if they want to do so. It's hardly fair, though, to ask the Church to lessen, weaken, and adapt its beliefs simply because they don't fit in with a person's circumstances, however difficult they may be. The same applies to who can and cannot receive the Eucharist, which causes many non-Catholics, even those who are fine and observant Christians, a great deal of discomfort. Catholics take the Eucharist extremely seriously because it is extremely serious. If it's not the body and blood of Jesus Christ, it doesn't really matter, and if it doesn't really matter, why bother to receive it and worry about not being able to receive it? If, however, it is the body and blood of Christ – as was demonstrated in an earlier chapter – the Church has to be extremely careful about it and particularly protective of it. Communion is the most personal encounter with God that we have, the taking into our bodies of our Messiah. It's not just those outside of the Church who are not supposed to receive Catholic communion but those inside the Church who are not prepared, not ready, or not in a correct state. That is, if you are not *in communion* with the body of Christ – His Church – then you should not *receive communion* with Him in the Eucharistic. Catholics must, first of all, be in communion with the Church's belief in the truth of the Eucharist. This might sound obvious but think again. There are those who self-identify as Catholics who do not genuinely believe in transubstantiation but as matter of convenience or to satisfy their friends and family or to fit in and not stand out go forward to receive the sacrament. This is wrong. And to participate without belief is a very serious matter indeed.

Sin breaks communion with God, and so Catholics must also be in a state of grace and must have been to confession if they have committed a mortal sin. There are almost always priests available to hear a confession, and even if it takes a little effort to find a priest it is hardly a major sacrifice compared with the sacrifice made by Christ and the gift He gives us in communion. Catholics must also abstain from food and drink other than water or medicine for at least an hour before receiving the sacrament. They should, of course, also pray before and afterwards and participate fully in the Mass and in the meaning of what is happening – which is a miracle available to all of us every day and almost everywhere. Do many Catholics take the Eucharist for granted? Of course. That is a human failing and a human reality, and human failings and human realities are why we need the Roman Catholic Church.

If Catholics disqualify themselves, it's their own fault and they should know better, but for faithful Christians who are not Catholic, the situation is more complex. Other denominations see their version of communion as a form of hospitality and friendship or as a type of communal meal and worship service where everyone is welcome. Everyone is also most welcome to attend Mass but not to receive communion. This is seen by some as being non-Christian and even anti-Christian – how dare one believer prevent another believer from being a full member of any gathering? Catholics, however, don't view this as a hospitality issue but as one of communion with the Catholic Church, and we cannot be in communion with the Catholic Church unless we are a member of it. It's rather like a marriage. The Eucharist is intimate and real and uniting and is part of a wedding to the Church. Those participating in it are participating in a form of marriage with the bishops and the Pope on earth and with the angels and saints in heaven. It would be rude to invite non-Catholics to take part. If people want to become Catholic, no one is more happy than a sincere and serious member of the Church so it's not about exclusion but about what it means to be Catholic. Anglicans, for example, do not enjoy the apostolic succession and cannot trace their origins and their priesthood back to Christ. While some of them, and in particular High Anglicans, may find their communion service deeply moving and may be committed Christians, it is not the Catholic sacrament, and they have specifically rejected that sacrament by not being Catholic. Other Protestants often do not regard communion as anything more than a symbol and it would be nothing short of offensive – both to them and to Catholics – if they were offered it or accepted it. In a perfect world, some argue, everybody would be entitled to the Catholic Eucharist. In a way I suppose that is true, because in a perfect world everybody would be Roman Catholic.

Any other strange accusations that Catholics confront? How about the flogging by some pseudo-historians of the conspiracy to bury the story of Pope Joan? If they were real historians, they would have understood Catholic history, and they would know that the scurrilous and silly accusation that there was a female Pope is merely urban myth. That, of course, hasn't stopped stage plays and movies being made and the odd, very odd, book being written about the so-called Pope Joan. This one is as much Monty Python as is nobody expecting the Spanish Inquisition but, believe it or not, far less plausible and convincing. Unless, of course, nobody in the ninth century could tell the difference between a man and a woman. Something of a transgendered fantasy, it's French farce disguised as Greek tragedy used as anti-Catholic drama. The story probably had its origins in the thirteenth century and was used before the Reformation by Catholics critical of the Church. Protestants after the Reformation were obviously even more critical of Catholicism, and they and assorted secularists and atheists have kept the tale alive. It is supposed to have begun in Mainz, Germany, with a clever, gifted girl who convinced everyone in a monastery that she was a he. She was a brilliant student, travelled to Athens, found a lover – who presumably discovered that she was a woman or was simply terribly confused – and then made it to Rome, still disguised and apparently convincing everyone around that she was a man. She became a secretary in the papal curia or civil service and then, as happened to all good cross-dressers in those days, was elected Pope in AD 855. Alas, the Church was not to be reformed and brought kicking and screaming into the modern tenth century because poor Pope

Joan was kicking and screaming as she felt her baby move in her womb. Not enjoying the contemporary gifts of cheap contraceptives or publicly funded abortion, the good lady was found out at long last and was killed by stoning or being dragged by a horse through the streets. Nobody is quite sure. This led to the awful Catholic Church insisting that all priests from then on had to be celibate and also to a persecution of women in the Church who in any way were too spiritual or who showed signs of achieving greatness in the Church. Simple really.

Except that there is no truth to it at all and, like so many children's stories, depends on a credulity and a suspension of disbelief and an absence of intelligent inquiry that is beyond even most Catholic-bashers. As we have already seen, priestly celibacy existed from the days of the early Church, and women were given power and influence in the Church that they would not have in the non-Catholic world for hundreds of years. The *Catholic Encyclopaedia* states, "Not one contemporaneous historical source among the papal histories knows anything about her; also, no mention is made of her until the middle of the thirteenth century. Now it is incredible that the appearance of a 'popess,' if it was an historical fact, would be noticed by none of the numerous historians from the tenth to the thirteenth century." Incredible it is.

There are similar legends in Roman mythology, and the stuff of women dressing as men is a common theme in Renaissance drama. The story would probably have been forgotten if it hadn't been used by anti-papal writers and then some of the reformers in the sixteenth century who were willing to use almost any ammunition to fire at the Church. Ironically enough, it was a vehement critic of Catholicism who confirmed that Pope Joan and her early feminist struggle against the patriarchy was an insult to intelligence. David Blondel lived through the Thirty Years War and saw the worst aspects of religious conflict. He was a Protestant clergyman, living in Protestant Holland and surrounded by Protestant ideas and Protestant friends. He was also a gifted historian who refused to allow propaganda to interfere with truth and by unpacking the Pope Joan myth concluded that it was a much later invention concocted by people with a vested interest in damaging the reputation of the papacy. There is no gap, he said, that Pope Joan could have filled because although she is said to have reigned between AD 855 and AD 877, Pope Leo IV died in June AD 855 and was immediately succeeded by Pope Benedict III. Quite a lot is known about this early election because the Byzantine Emperor tried to influence the outcome. The more we have learned about history and the more we learned how to use and apply history, the more we have realized that this story was a product of a drunken imagination. It's amazing, though, how many allegedly sober journalists and filmmakers choose lies over truth.

Lastly to hypocrites. It seems a sad way to conclude a book but perhaps it is fitting that this subject should be at the rear of such a work. To give hypocrites their most descriptive titles: politicians, powerful people, and even ordinary men and women who claim to be Roman Catholic but behave as if they weren't. Being Catholic does have a cultural context, and while many people struggle and evolve in their Catholic faith, the mere fact of being born to Catholic parents or in a Catholic country is not enough. Being Catholic is not the same as being Jewish, for example, in that Judaism has a secular aspect and there are Jewish people who describe themselves as atheists who are still to a large degree accepted within the Jewish community. Both the friends and, sadly, the enemies of

Judaism have guaranteed that Jewish identity is not as straightforward as religious belief. Catholicism is different. But anyone who listens to public discourse will hear people criticizing or mocking Catholic teaching while defending or justifying their comments with the explanation that they are Catholic too so it's okay, often followed by some joke about Catholic school, a joke about a priest, or some nonsense about the size of a Catholic next-door-neighbour's family. This is irritating but relatively unimportant. More problematic are politicians who campaign against and vote against Catholic teaching but insist on announcing, particularly at election time, that they are faithful Catholics and that being Catholic sometimes means taking issue with the Church. In fact, they are usually not Catholic, not faithful, and not taking issue. They are exploiting their nominal Catholicism for their own ends. As politicians they can say and do whatever they want, but as Catholics they should speak and act as members of the Church.

When, however, bishops, cardinals, or parish priests rebuke them, the response of the politician and their friends in the media is generally to tell the Church to keep out of politics. Good Lord, reality cries out to be heard. It's not the Church interfering in politics but politicians interfering in the Church. If a politician claims to be a Catholic, a priest has an obligation to guide that person to God and heaven, and the regular and repeated political support for propositions that contradict Church teaching and Christian belief will take the politician in the opposite direction. It's an act of kindness and not aggression for a clergyman to try to help a politician save his soul, even at the expense of losing his political career. These men and women ought to learn from the lesson of St. Thomas More and his martyrdom due to his refusal to deny Church teaching, his refusal to agree to an end to papal supremacy, and his support for genuine marriage. One can stand in the man's last dwelling-space – the cell in the Tower of London – and appreciate in the harsh, compellingly beautiful but coldly unforgiving room the contemporary resonance of More's heroism when we compare him as a statesman to those men and women in international politics who claim to be Catholic but work and vote against fundamental Catholic doctrine. They do so with the usual chant that we must separate church and state and that their personal views must not influence their public policies, one of the most disingenuous utterances ever to bruise the body politic.

Truth is not geographical. If it's true in a church or a home, it's true in a parliament or a courtroom. If it's true, it's true. If unborn life is sacred, if marriage can only be between a man and a woman, if unjust war is wrong, if exploitation of the poor and weak is immoral, it's always the case. We would think little of a man who loved his wife when in his home country but was unfaithful to her when on vacation. Or someone who told the truth to one person but an untruth to another. The first is an adulterer, the second a liar. On the abortion and marriage issues in particular, it is not that ostensibly Catholic politicians have found the matters complex but that they have found them inconvenient. But if it's a life or a sacrament, it's not trivial, it's not a fashion statement, it's not something mutable and passing like a party platform position. If they're genuinely Catholic, they should be ashamed; if they're just cultural Catholics, they should have the courage to admit the truth. What so much of it all comes down to, of course, are men and women not living out their Catholic faith. They also failed during Thomas More's era, when legions of politicians, priests, prelates, and people gave in and gave up. That was for the sake of their lives.

Today politicians do the same for the sake of their limousines. It would be easier to take if they just told us that their careers were in danger if they voted for the Catholic rather than the party line. Instead they obfuscate with arguments about church and state separation and representing all and not just some of their constituents, supporters, and voters. Nonsense! It's long been established that an elected politician is not a mere delegate and is elected to guide as well as represent. On the subject of the death penalty, for example, it may well be that the majority of the elected official's voters support capital punishment but few of them would then feel obliged to vote for hanging. This is about pleasing media rather than the masses.

When it comes to the separation of church and state, this is an American concept that doesn't apply to every country and anyway concerns the protection of the freedom of individual Christians rather than the threat of the interference of Christian ethics into national politics. Anybody who does not understand that does not understand the history of Protestant ministers or Catholic priests and nuns building public hospitals and establishing free education. Thomas More loved life, was not physically brave, and had so much for which to live. But he had more for which to die: truth and the Church, two concepts that are as important now as they were in the sixteenth century. And Catholicism is as important now as it ever was and perhaps even more necessary in a world that appears to prefer confusion to clarity and to long for feelings instead of facts. All sorts of people have interesting and valuable ideas and deserve to be heard. Catholics particularly so. Because Catholics are right.

ACKNOWLEDGMENTS

Numerous people have helped me write this book – some of them by their learning and their ability to teach truth and others by their lack of learning and their ability, sometimes unwittingly, to teach the nature of error. To both groups of people I owe a great debt of gratitude. The latter shall remain nameless because it would be unfair to embarrass them and, anyway, they tend to receive far too much attention already. The former especially include Anthony Schratz and Fr. Stefano Penna, both of whom gave expert advice and guidance. To my publisher at McClelland & Stewart, Doug Pepper, and to my editor, Jenny Bradshaw, I owe a great deal; eternal thanks to Monsignor Frederick Miles, the man who instructed and then received me into the Roman Catholic Church in 1985. Finally, of course, to my wife, Bernadette, and to my children, Daniel, Lucy, Oliver, and Elizabeth, I owe more than I can ever say.

N O T E S

INTRODUCTION

1. Philip Jenkins, *The New Anti-Catholicism* (Oxford, 2004).
2. Jeremy Lott, Philip Jenkins:*The Wittenburg Door Interview*, October 2005 (http://archives.wittenburgdoor.com/archives/philipjenkins.html).

CHAPTER ONE – Catholics and the Abuse Scandal

1. Philip Jenkins, *Pedophiles and Priests* (Oxford, 2001).
2. Ibid.
3. Neil Dale, *Asheville Citizen Times*, May 14, 2002.
4. Cal Thomas, *Baltimore Sun*, June 19, 2002.
5. Jenkins, *Pedophiles and Priests*.
6. Mark Clayton, *Christian Science Monitor*, April 2002.
7. www.rrc.edu/journal, November 24, 2003.
8. Jenkins, *Pedophiles and Priests*.
9. Ibid.
10. Ibid.
11. Catholic League for Religious and Civil Rights, *Sexual Abuse in Social Context: Catholic Clergy and Other Professionals*, February 2004 (http://www.catholicleague.org/research/abuse_in_social_context.htm).
12. John R. Willis, *The Teachings of the Church Fathers* (Ignatius Press, 2002).

13. Carl J. Sommer, *We Look for a Kingdom* (Ignatius Press, 2007).

CHAPTER TWO – Catholics and History

1. Rodney Stark, *God's Battalions* (Harper, 2009).
2. Steven Runciman, *A History of the Crusades* (Cambridge, 1951).
3. Stark, *God's Battalions*.
4. Ibid.
5. Carl J. Sommer, *We Look for a Kingdom* (Ignatius Press, 2007).
6. Jonathan Phillips, *Holy Warriors* (Random House, 2009).
7. Runciman, *A History of the Crusades*.
8. Sean McGlynn, *By Sword and Fire* (Weidenfeld & Nicolson, 2008).
9. Christopher Tyerman, God's War (Penguin, 2006).
10. Runciman, *A History of the Crusades*.
11. Henry Charles Lea, *History of the Inquisition of the Middle Ages* (New York, 1888).
12. Warren H. Carroll, *A History of Christendom* (Christendom Press, 1987).
13. George Weigel, *Witness to Hope* (Harper Collins, 1999).
14. Carroll, *A History of Christendom*.
15. Philip Hughes, *A History of the Church* (Sheed & Ward, 1947).
16. *Elizabeth*, 1998, and *Elizabeth: The Golden Age*, 2007.
17. Carroll, *A History of Christendom*.
18. Neill Schmandt, *History of the Catholic Church* (Bruce Publishing, 1957).
19. Thomas E. Woods Jr., *How the Catholic Church Built Western Civilization* (Regnery, 2005).
20. Jonathan Wright, *God's Soldiers* (Doubleday, 2004).
21. Carroll, *A History of Christendom*.
22. Robert Conquest, *The Great Terror: A Reassessment* (Oxford, 1977).

23. Sir Martin Gilbert, *The Righteous* (Key Porter, 2003).
24. Rabbi David G. Dalin, *The Myth of Hitler's Pope* (Regnery, 2005).
25. Ibid.
26. Ibid.
27. Ibid.
28. Dan Kurzman, *A Special Mission* (Da Capo, 2007).
29. Pinchas Lapide, *Three Popes and the Jews* (Souvenir Press, 1967).
30. Dalin, *The Myth of Hitler's Pope*.
31. Simon Caldwell, *The Daily Telegraph*, July 7, 2010.
32. Ibid.

CHAPTER THREE – Catholics and Theology

1. Stephen K. Ray, *Upon This Rock* (Ignatius, 1999).
2. Ibid.
3. John R. Willis, *The Teachings of the Church Fathers* (Ignatius Press, 2002).
4. Ibid.
5. *Vatican Council II: The Conciliar and Postconciliar Documents* (Costello Publishing, 1975).
6. Charles A. Coulombie, *A History of the Popes* (MJF Books, 2003).
7. Willis, *The Teachings of the Church Fathers*.
8. Ibid.
9. Carroll, *A History of Christendom*.
10. Craig Blomberg, *The Historical Reliability of the Gospels* (Downers Grove, 1987).
11. *Catholic Encylopedia, 1907–1912* (Robert Appleton Company).
12. Philip Hughes, *A History of the Church* (Sheed & Ward, 1947).
13. Peter Stravinskas, *The Catholic Church and the Bible* (Ignatius, 1996).

14. Carl J. Sommer, *We Look for a Kingdom* (Ignatius Press, 2007).

15. Willis, *The Teachings of the Church Fathers*.

16. Glenn W. Olsen, *Beginning at Jerusalem* (Ignatius, 2004).

17. Willis, *The Teachings of the Church Fathers*.

18. Ibid.

19. Kenneth L. Woodward, *Making Saints* (Touchstone, 1996).

20. Willis, *The Teachings of the Church Fathers*.

21. Warren H. Carroll, *A History of Christendom* (Christendom Press, 1987).

22. Dwight Longenecker and David Gustafson, *Mary* (Gracewing, 2003).

23. Kenneth D. Whitehead, *One, Holy, Catholic, and Apostolic* (Ignatius, 2000).

CHAPTER FOUR – Catholics and Life

1. Dr. Brian Clowes, *The Facts of Life* (HLI, 1997).

2. Robert P. George and Christopher Tollefsen, *Embryo: A Defence of Human Life* (Doubleday, 2008).

3. Scott Klusendorf, *The Case for Life* (Crossway, 2009).

4. Ibid.

5. Ibid.

6. U.N. Population Database, 2008.

7. Food and Agriculture Organisation, UN, 2007.

8. Jacqueline Kasun, *War Against Population* (Ignatius, 1988).

9. John Paul II, *The Theology of the Body* (Pauline, 1997).

10. Breast Cancer (OMS, 2000) Dr. Chris Kahlenborn

11. Clowes, *The Facts of Life*.

12. John Carey, *The Intellectuals and the Masses* (London, 1992).

CHAPTER FIVE – Catholics and Other Stuff

1. Paul J. Maier, *Josephus: The Essential Works* (Kregel, 1988).
2. Craig Blomberg, *The Historical Reliability of the Gospels* (Downers Grove, 1987).
3. Ibid.
4. John L. Allen, *Opus Dei: An Objective Look Behind the Myths and Reality of the Most Controversial Force in the Catholic Church* (Doubleday, 2005).
5. James L. Garlow, *The Da Vinci Code Breaker* (Bethany House, 2006).
6. Allen, *Opus Dei* (Doubleday, 2005).
7. Warren H. Carroll, *A History of Christendom* (Christendom Press, 1987).
8. Willis, *The Teachings of the Church Fathers.*

B I B L I O G R A P H Y

There are various authors whose entire body of work is essential reading. From the distant past there are the Church fathers. From the medieval age there is, at the very least, St. Thomas Aquinas. From the nineteenth and earlier twentieth centuries there are, to name but a few, Hilaire Belloc, G.K. Chesterton, Cardinal Newman, Ronald Knox, Alfred Lunn, and C.S. Lewis. The latter wasn't a Catholic but his defence of Christianity is unparalleled and, as his friend the great Walter Hooper argues, "he was Catholic in all but name and certainly would have been a member of the Church today." From the modern age we have Scott Hahn, Fr. Ian Ker, George Weigel, Stephen Ray, Karl Keating, Patrick Madrid, but there are many more than these. The challenge with Catholic books and Catholic authors is not that they are too few but that they are so many.

This list of books is neither exhaustive nor exhausting. It is brief and selective. Think of it as a stone thrown into the great lake of Catholic literature—the ripples will extend to the most extraordinary places.

CHAPTER ONE – Catholics and the Abuse Scandal

Erlandson, Gregory, and Matthew Bunson. Pope *Benedict XVI and the Sexual Abuse Crisis* (Our Sunday Visitor, 2010).
Jenkins, Philip. *Pedophiles and Priests* (Oxford, 2001).

Weigel, George. *The Courage to Be Catholic* (Basic, 2002).

CHAPTER TWO – Catholics and History

Burleigh, Michael. *Earthly Powers* (Harper Collins, 2005).

———. *Sacred Causes* (Harper Collins, 2007).

Carroll, Warren. *A History of Christendom*, 5 vols. (Christendom Press, 1987–2010).

Chesterton, G.K. *The Everlasting Man* (Ignatius, 1993).

Dalin, Rabbi David G. *The Myth of Hitler's Pope* (Regnery, 2005).

Daniel-Rops, H. *The Church in an Age of Revolution* (Dent, 1965).

Duffy, Eamon. *The Stripping of the Altars* (Yale, 2005).

Hogge, Alice. *God's Agents* (2006, Harper).

Kurzman, Dan. *A Special Mission* (Da Capo, 2007).

Sommer, Carl J. *We Look for a Kingdom* (Ignatius, 2007).

Waugh, Evelyn. *Edmund Campion* (Ignatius, 2005).

Weigel, George. *Witness to Hope* (Collins, 1999).

Woods, Thomas E. *How the Catholic Church Built Western Civilization* (Regnery, 2005).

Zolli, Eugenio. *Before the Dawn* (Sheed & Ward, 1954).

CHAPTER THREE – Catholics and Theology

Armstrong, Regis. *Writings for a Gospel Life* (St. Paul's, 1994).

Balthasar, Hans Urs von. *Dare We Hope That All Men Be Saved?* (Ignatius, 1988).

Catechism of the Catholic Church (Chapman, 1994).

Chesterton, G.K. *Heretics* (1905, London).

Crean, Thomas. *A Catholic Replies to Professor Dawkins* (Family Publications, 2007).

Gilbey, Monsignor A.N. *We Believe* (The Saint Austin Press, 2003).

Guarducci, Margherita. *The Primacy of the Church of Rome* (Ignatius, 2003).

Knox, Ronald. *The Belief of Catholics* (London, 1927).

Kreeft, Peter. *The Snakebite Letters* (Ignatius, 1991).

Pham, John-Peter. *Heirs of the Fisherman* (Oxford, 2004).

Sheed, Frank. *Theology and Sanity* (Ignatius, 1978).

Willis, John R. *The Teachings of the Church Fathers* (Ignatius, 2002).

Weigel, George. *Letters to a Young Catholic* (2006, Gracewing).

CHAPTER FOUR – Catholics and Life

Blankenhorn, David. *The Future of Marriage* (Encounter, 2007).

Clowes, Dr. Brian. *The Facts of Life* (HLI, 1997).

Coffin, Patrick. *Sex Au Naturel* (Emmaus Road, 2010).

George, Robert P., and Christopher Tollefsen. *Embryo: A Defence of Human Life* (Doubleday, 2008).

John Paul II. *The Theology of the Body* (Pauline, 1997).

Kahlenborn, Dr. Chris. *Breast Cancer* (OMS, 2000).

Klusendorf, Scott. *The Case for Life* (Crossway, 2009).

Nathanson, Bernard N. *Abortion Papers: Inside the Abortion Mentality* (Frederick Fell, 1983).

———. *The Hand of God: A Journey from Death to Life by the Abortion Doctor Who Changed His Mind* (Regnery, 2001).

Reisman, Dr. Judith A. *Kinsey: Crimes and Consequences* (The Institute for Media Education, 2000).

CHAPTER FIVE – Catholics and Other Stuff

Allen, John L., Jr. *Opus Dei* (Doubleday, 2005).

Chaput, Charles J. *Render Unto Caesar* (Doubleday, 2008).

D'Souza, Dinesh. *What's So Great About Christianity* (Regnery, 2007).

Jones, E. Michael. *Degenerate Moderns* (Ignatius, 1993).

Keating, Karl. *Catholicism and Fundamentalism* (Ignatius, 1988).

Ker, Fr. Ian. *Mere Catholicism* (Emmaus Road, 2006).

Longenecker, Dwight. *More Christianity* (Our Sunday Visitor, 2002).

Madrid, Patrick. *Pope Fiction* (Basilica, 2005).

——. *Why Is That in Tradition* (Our Sunday Visitor, 2002).

Muggeridge, Anne Roche. *The Desolate City* (McClelland & Stewart, 1986).

Muggeridge, Malcolm. *Something Beautiful for God* (Collins, 1997).

Nichols, Aidan. *Christendom Awake* (Eerdmans, 1999).

Ripley, Canon Francis. *This Is the Faith* (TAN, 2002).

Rumble, Fr., and Fr. Carty. *Radio Replies*, 3 vols. (TAN, 1979).